WHO WAS WHO 5000 B. C. to Date

Biographical Dictionary of the

Famous and Those Who Wanted to Be

Edited by Irwin L. Gordon

First published in 1914

Published by Left of Brain Books

Copyright © 2023 Left of Brain Books

ISBN 978-1-396-32440-6

First Edition

All rights reserved. No part of this publication may be reproduced, distributed, or transmitted in any form or by any means, including photocopying, recording, or other electronic or mechanical methods, without the prior written permission of the publisher, except in the case of brief quotations permitted by copyright law. Left of Brain Books is a division of Left Of Brain Onboarding Pty Ltd.

PUBLISHER'S PREFACE

About the Book

A biographical dictionary of famous people from the beginning of recorded history, up until 1914.

CONTENTS

PUBLISHER'S PREFACE NOTE 1
ABBREVIATIONS 2
OBITUARY 4
    CHAPTER A 6
    CHAPTER B 11
    CHAPTER C 19
    CHAPTER D 27
    CHAPTER E 33
    CHAPTER F 36
    CHAPTER G 39
    CHAPTER H 44
    CHAPTER I 50
    CHAPTER J 52
    CHAPTER K 56
    CHAPTER L 58
    CHAPTER M 64
    CHAPTER N 70
    CHAPTER O 74
    CHAPTER P 76
    CHAPTER Q 82
    CHAPTER R 83
    CHAPTER S 89
    CHAPTER T 96
    CHAPTER U 100
    CHAPTER V 101
    CHAPTER W 103
    CHAPTER X 106
    CHAPTER Y 107
    CHAPTER Z 108

NOTE

The editor begs leave to inform the public that only persons who can produce proper evidence of their demise will be admitted to Who Was Who. Press Agent notices or complimentary comments are absolutely excluded, and those offering to pay for the insertion of names will be prosecuted. As persons become eligible they will be included without solicitation, while the pages will be expurgated of others should good luck warrant.

Who Was Who contains over 500 biographies of those who did or endeavored to become famous. In a work of such magnitude errors occasionally occur. Should this be the case, the editor will be glad to receive corrections from the ex-celebrities or their enemies. These will be accepted gratis. Proofs will be sent to all subscribers. Members of the family will be able to order the coming editions in advance by applying and remitting to the publisher.

The work is fully protected by the libel laws of the United States and Great Britain. Under no circumstance will duels be fought.

The editor wishes to express his thanks to those who have furnished material for this book. He also trusts they will show their good feeling by purchasing a copy, and that all the unfortunates will speedily be returned to Who's Who.

THE EDITOR.

ABBREVIATIONS

A1.......... Can open charge account.
A. B........ Four years hard sentence.
A. M........ When we get up.
Cit......... Common people.
C. O. D..... No credit.
Cong........ A Washington organization used for social and investigation purposes.
D. D........ Be careful of your jokes.
Dem......... Politicians who get in office, once in awhile.
D. H........ Pull.
D. T........ Delirium tremens.
Ets......... The rest of us.
F. R. A..... Brains.
F. R. G. S.. People who do not stay at home.
G. O. P..... Hic jacet.
Hon......... Speaker of the occasion.
H. R. H..... Chief advertiser for cigarettes, mustard and kid gloves.
I........... Roosevelt.
Incog....... Prominent men in Paris.
IOU......... Hard luck.
Ire......... Mother of politicians.
LL. D....... American millionaires.
M. P........ Home rule debaters.
Parl........ Where the M. P.s debate.
P. M........ When we go to bed.
R. A........ Any kind of a painter but a cubist.
Rep......... See G. O. P.
R. I. P..... See following pages.

Sir......... Writers and tea merchants.
U. S. A..... Bryan + Wilson.

OBITUARY

Bryan, William Jennings, of U. S. A.
Cannon, Joseph G., of U. S. Congress.
Castro, Cipriano, of Venezuela Asphalt Trust.
Cavalieri, Lina, of Paris and New York City.
Cook, Doctor Fred. A., of New York City and Denmark.
Dewey, George E., of U. S. N.
Diaz, Perfiro, of Mexico.
Din, Gunga, of Kipling.
Dreyfus, Captain, of France.
Fallieres, Armand, of the French Republic.
Gorky, Maxime, of Russia.
Hafid, Mulai, of Morocco.
Hamed, Abdul, of Turkey.
Hammerstein, Oscar, of New York City and London.
Holmes, Sherlock, of Doyle.
Huerta, V., General of Mexico.
Irish Home Rule, of Ireland and London.
Johnson, Jack, of U. S. A.
Lloyd-George, David, of England.
Manuel, King, of Portugal.
Pankhurst, Mrs., of England.
Patti, Adelina, of Wales.
Roberts, Frederick S., of Kandohr.
Rojesvensky, Admiral, of Russia.
Roosevelt, Theodore, of "The Outlook."
Shackelton, Earnest, of England.
Shuster, Morgan, of Persia.
Sulzer, William, of Tammany Fall.
Taft, William Howard, of Cincinnati, U. S. A.

Time, Father, of Everywhere.
Turkey.
Widow, Merry, of Paris, London, and New York City.

CHAPTER A

ADAM[1] (last name unknown), ancestor, explorer, gardener, and inaugurator of history. Biographers differ as to his parentage. Born first Saturday of year 1. Little is known of his childhood. Education: Self-educated. Entered the gardening and orchard business when a young man. Was a strong anti-polygamist. Married Eve, a close relative. Children, Cain and Abel (see them). Was prosperous for some years, but eventually fell prey to his wife's fruitful ambitions. Lost favor of the proprietor of the garden, and failed in business. A. started a number of things which have not been perfected. Diet: Fond of apples. Recreation: Chess, agriculture. Address: Eden, General Delivery. Clubs: Member of all exclusive clubs.

ABEL, son of the above. Spent early days in the Garden of Eden with his parents, and later traveled with them. Conducted a sheep raising business. Finally had a row with his brother, and was knocked out in the first round.

ABRAHAM, a patriarch whose descendants now own New York City, Jerusalem, vast sections of the remainder of the globe, and control the pawn-broking, diamond, theatrical, and old clothing markets. Camel and sheep merchant. Considerable land was willed him. A. prospered. Married Sarah (last name unknown). Marital infelicity followed, A. having an affair with Mrs. Abraham's maid. The woman was discharged, and the family lived happily ever afterward. Ambition: The chosen people.

---

[1] Ed. Note: Adam should not be first, but he is given that position out of respect.

Recreation: Riding, tennis, camel racing. Address: Caanan. Clubs: Country.

ABRUSSI, Prince Luigi Amedeo Guiseppe Maria Ferdinando Francesco, of the Italian nobility. Spent the greater portion of his life taking care of his name, climbing mountains, fighting Turks, and denying rumors regarding his marriage.

ACHILLES (first name unknown), a baby whose mother gave him a bath, but forgot to wash all of his feet. Later was veteran of the siege of Troy. Died before receiving pension.

AESOP, novelist, nature faker. Little is known of his childhood except that he was fond of dogs and played with the cat. Later he made animals his life's study. A. discovered the zoological principal that a turtle can run faster than a rabbit, and that foxes never eat sour grapes. Publications: Fables; the book has had a good sale. Address: Greece. Clubs: Zoological Societies.

ALADDIN, of Somewhere. An ancient who possessed a lamp and a genii with which he could secure anything an American millionaire or actress can now purchase.

ALDRICH, Senator N. W., architect of the Aldrich Plan, a system for removing the financial interests of the country from the common people and placing them in the hands of the few.

ALPHONSO XIII, a king who enjoyed Paris without losing his job.

AMUNDSON, Captain Roald, another pole discoverer. Away back in the year 1912 he reached the south pole after a considerable journey through the Arctic regions. Like his predecessors he became an author and lecturer. Publications: The South Pole. Price, Pd2.2S in England; $10.50 in the U. S.

Later A. retired and lived on his royalty. Ambition: A few more poles, a few more books.

ANANIAS. See Dr. Cook and Roosevelt.

ANDERSON, Mary, actress; one of the wisest women who ever lived. In the height of a brilliant stage career she fell in love, and decided that a quiet home with a husband and children was more to be desired than the empty plaudits of the crowd, and the attentions of stage-door Johnnies.

ANGELO, Mike, painter and sculptor of no mean ability. Born in Italy, but named after Irish relatives. At school he showed his talents by making cartoons of the teachers. These were unappreciated. Moved to Florence, where he bought some chisels, brushes, and saw his first model. A. remained a bachelor. Later he moved to Rome, and began a brilliant church-decorating career. Secured permission of the Pope to give an exhibition in the Vatican. This was finally made permanent. Also made a fortune erecting tomb-stones for the Medici family, leading politicians of his time. It is difficult to leave Italy without seeing much of his work. A. never favored the cubists or post-impressionists. Recreations: Painting, sculpture. Address: Rome.

ANTHONY, Saint, of Pauda. An Italian who visited Paris, and could not forget what he saw.

ANTOINETTE, Marie, wife of Louis No. 15, who assisted her husband to spend the French taxes. Was also a practical joker, her humor terminating at Versailles when she advised a mob to eat cake during a bread famine. Her wit was unappreciated. Ambition: Anything but October 16, 1791. Recreation: Versailles; looking through a grated window. Address: Versailles. Later: Consiergerie, Paris.

APOLLO, a handsome ancient who fell in love, posed for his statues, patronized music and poetry, and, finally, had a table water named in his honor. Career: See longer and less respectable biographies. A. was the first person to sing to the accompaniment of a musical instrument, but he was a good singer. Ambition: Paris. Recreation: Music, travel, archery. Address: Greece. Clubs: Athletic, musical.

ARC, Joan of, celebrated French suffragette. Spent girlhood milking cows and embroidering. When the English ministry began operations in France J. dropped her embroidery in the milk bucket and began suffragetting. She did not break windows or blow up anything. Gathered a host of males about her and captured towns. English exited. J. went back to the cow, but again had to take to the armor. She was finally jailed, and burnt up by the Radical ministry. She burned an old maid. Recreation: Barn dances, churning. Clubs: Orleans Suffragette.

ARISTOTLE. Introduced brains into Greece.

ARMOUR, a Chicago family who keep the world supplied with meat, and themselves out of the government jails.

ARNOLD, Benedict, a man who sent his name down through history with a bad odor attached to it.

ARTHUR, King, a very dead English sovereign who manufactured the Round Table, and did all the things a good English king should do. Little is known of his Prince of Waleshood. Was crowned in Westminster Abbey, but without the American contingent. Became proficient as a knight. Stayed away from the palace so much his queen began flirting. Al's sword was a wonder. Press Agent: Lord Tennyson. recreation: Grailing. Address: Windsor, Buckingham.

ASQUITH, Herbert Henry, an Englishman who helped run things in his country before 1908, and who ran things after 1908. Was also a favorite rallying point for suffragettes. Led a successful wing-dipping expedition against some of his countrymen who held titles to names and property. Also juggled dynamite in Parliament (see Lloyd-George). Ambition: Women without ambitions. Recreation: Dodging, golf. Address: Constantly in danger of a change. Clubs: Favored Radical.

ATKINS, Thomas, celebrated red-coat-wearing dandy who flirts with nurses and cooks, spends his time boasting about South Africa and the U. S. A., posing for motion pictures, and exhibiting royalty. Authorities differ as to his marksmanship, although it is now conceded he can often hit a man-sized target at the distance of 4 feet 3 inches. Weather, however, must be clear. Is an authority on creases, backbone, accent, and tea. Beverage: Everything. Recreation: Jacks, collecting stamps, Kipling, blindman's-buff, parlor tricks, May-pole festivities. Ambition: Tortoise-shell monocles, camp manacurists, pocket bath-tubs, and restoration of the tea canteen. Epitaph: See Emperor William.

ATLAS, a man who held up the heavens and was not even a preacher. Edited a huge book which bears his name.

AURELIUS, Marcus, one of the few Romans who is not remembered for crossing a river, for being murdered, for murdering somebody, for making speeches, or building triumphant arches or ruins.

CHAPTER B

BABY, T. H. E., an unscrupulous tyrant, s. father and mother. His first appearance caused heaven at home, and an idiotic father. Education: At home. Career: A series of adventures. Was frequently ill, a poor sleeper, toy demolisher, throat exerciser, nurse distractor, and a general nuisance. Despite his shortcomings he ruled Home with an iron hand--a tear caused a doctor--a smile meant a gold mine. Diet: Principally liquid. Ambition: The moon. Recreation: Coaching, hair pulling, a proud father. Address: See Mother.

BACCHUS, patron saint of most men, benefactor, a jolly good fellow, and the founder of the "morning after" feeling. Studied vine raising when a young man. Discovered that grapes were not intended for a food. Invented the greatest pleasure and pain giver the world has ever seen. Became a traveler. Introduced ale and stout in England, whiskey in Scotland, everything in Ireland, cocktails and patent medicines in the United States, beer in Germany, champagne in France, absinthe in France, and vodka in Russia. Career: Magnificent. Recreation: Paris. Address: Greece. Clubs: All, except W. C. T. U. Epitaph: He Will Live In The Throats Of His Countrymen.

BACON, Francis, either wrote or did not write Shakespeare.

BAEDEKER, Karl, one of the most versatile men who ever lived. Childhood and old age unknown. Formed an ambition to travel when quite young. First visited Switzerland, where he climbed every peak, walked every path, hired every guide, and did everything a tourist should so. His field of travel widened until every country in Europe was visited, as well as the United States, Canada, Alaska, and Mexico. In these lands he slept in every hotel, ate every dish in every restaurant, drank every wine, rode on every boat, tramway, subway, and train; visited every ruin, museum, art gallery, church, store; mastered every language, science, art, literature, custom, history, and drew maps and plans of everything. Publications: Baedekers. Recreation: Staying at home. Ambition: Tourists. Residence: Germany.

BALFOUR, Arthur James, of England, one time leader of the talking forces of the House of Commons. Ambition: Opposition seats on both sides of the house, and an epitaph over the home rule bill. Recreation: St. Andrew's golf and writing deep books.

BALZAC, H., a Frenchman who wrote a few Parisian stories which may be discussed in respectable company.

BARBAROSSA, Kaiser, the only emperor of Germany who ever went to sleep.

BARKIS. Fame rested only upon his complete willingness.

BARLEYCORN, John, an eminent citizen of the world. Spent early days in the fields, breweries, and distilleries. Later resided in cellars. John had a red nose. Was a great friend of Bacchus. He was a "wasser," he is an "iser," and he will be a "will be-er." Ambition: The end of temperance societies.

BARNUM, Phineas T., fathered the introduction of the peanut, the clown, and the beautiful bareback riders. As a side show he taught that some Americans were Progressives part of the time; that other Americans were Republicans all the time, but that all Americans were not Democrats all the time.

BARRY, Madame Du, writers' model, former queen of France. Was a great friend of Louis XV. and helped make the dances at Versailles a success. She always preferred marcel waves to pompadours. Ambition: To have and to hold. Address: See Louis. Clubs: Anti-suffragette.

BARTHOLOMEW, an unfortunate saint who was skinned alive. Patron of gold mine investors and American tourists in Europe.

BEARD, Blue, inventor of an original method to dispose of wives, before Reno was discovered.

BEATRICE, a Florentine girl who gained fame by refusing the suit of a love-sick poet. Later she conducted him through heaven, and made arrangements for his travels in the other place. B. died a famous old maid. Ambition: A lover with money. Epitaph: She Might Have Been Mrs. Dante Had She Wanted To.

BEECHAM, a celebrated pill roller.

BELL, Alexander Graham, inventor of a well-known necessity and nuisance. Started the saying, "Number, please."

BELSHAZZAR, an old king whose handwriting on the wall proved to be correct.

BENEDICT, Saint, the man who introduced benedictine and monks into Europe. Also gave his name to benedicts.

BERLITZ, the man who will teach you how to say it in everything.

BERNHARDT, Sarah, an ancient French actress. Sarah was born before birth records were inaugurated, and no historian has been able to determine her age. Career: On the stage at four months. During her young-woman and goodlooking days-hood B. is said to have made a hit with European nobility. In her declining years she made a few other fortunes in the United States. B.'s fame culminated in having several cigars, perfumes, perspiration powders, and a theatre named after her. Ambition: The fountain of youth. Recreation: Statuary, acting. Address: Private cars and 56 Blvd. Pereire, Paris. She also has a telephone.

BILL, Buffalo, alias W. F. Cody, the delight of the American boy. He began his career shooting buffaloes and Indians on the plains of the West, and ended it shooting glass balls for a fortune in a tent. Installed the I-want-to-be-a-cow-boy ambition in the hearts of young America. He also made a goatee and a big hat famous. Played the show market a little too long.

BILLIKEN, a funny little fellow who did not wear many clothes, and made people laugh.

BISMARCK, a German who was a greater politician than any Ireland has ever produced. He built an empire, crowned an emperor, changed the Frenchmen in Alsace-Lorraine into Dutchmen, and made the Paris mint work overtime for his country. Quite unpopular in France. Ambition: Made in Germany.

BLACKSTONE, a rock upon which many a legal ship has foundered.

BLERIOT, benefactor of humanity, idol of the tourist, and enemy of navigation. B. discovered a method of crossing the English Channel without being seasick.

BLUCHER, a Dutchman who was on the job at Waterloo. He also was not the only German general who ever fought France.

BONAPARTE, Joe, just Nap.'s brother (see him).

BONHEUR, Rosa, a lady French artist who wore men's clothes. Being an old maid, she painted animals, but never mastered the parrot or the cat. Her endeavors were confined to horses, and one of her paintings is considered fair.

BOOTH, General William, founder of a vast army which never fought a battle, made a retreat, or surrendered. Conducted campaigns in Great Britain and the United States, with brass bands and collection devises. The army later became a suffragette institution when women were admitted as recruits, and placed as sentries to guard the Christmas-Easter collection forts. Publication: War Cry. Recreation: Reviewing troopers and troopesses.

BOSWELL, Dr. Johnson's press agent (see the Doctor).

BRADSTREET, author. Wrote a book in which he described your bank account and told how you paid your bills. His complimentary comments are highly valued.

BRIEUX, Eugene, a seller of damaged goods who got away with it without being fined or driven out of business.

BROWN, John, an American who helped start the Civil War by espousing the cause of the negro. This resulted in his body moulding in the grave.

BROWN, Thomas, an Englishman who reversed the usual procedure of life by springing into print when young, and keeping out of it when old.

BROWNING, Robert, a cryptogram writer whose poems are deciphered by the Bostonese and cultured English people. It has been estimated that B. could say more with fewer words and conceal his meaning better than any writer since the adaptation of the alphabet as a means of expression.

BROWNING, Mrs., Bob's wife. She also wrote poems. They were easily understood, and consequently seldom read.

BRUMMELL, Beau, a man whose thoughts were more for the crease in his pantaloons than for his head.

BRUTUS, Et Tu, a Roman murderer.

BRYAN, William Jennings, a famous Chatauqua lecturer who ran a newspaper and the State Department on the side. Archaeologists claim B. formed a passion to rule the nation when a child. He only got as far as the Democratic party and platforms. Became a golden orator with a silver speech and offered himself as a rectifier of all things not Bryan. For ages his name was placed on the presidential ballot and later removed. Made a fortune by telling people why they did not elect him. Also toured the world, but shot no game in Africa or Monte Carlo. Was the father of Bryanism, an odious word meaning things Bryan. Later secured one Wilson to attend to Washington detail work. Motto: All things come to him with bait. Ambition: Short ballot with one name. Publications: The Commoner, a newspaper devoted to Bryan advertisements. Address: Mail forwarded from Washington. Epitaph: He Will Rise Again.

BUCHANAN, J. C., manufacturer of the Scotchman's delight and weakness. He showed the world the excellence of two colors, and caused many a man to lose the keyhole.

BUDDHA, a prince of India who tired of good times and turned reformer. Advised his congregations to adopt the recall and referendum. Nailed several anti-saloon and burlesque planks in his platform. After B.'s death his friends filled the Orient with his bronzes. He was fat and wore a fascinating wart on his forehead.

BULL, John, a fine, fat, American-beef fed individual who inhabits a suffragette-infested island somewhere in the North Atlantic. Born several hundred years ago and is beginning to show his age. Is fond of the sea and is said to have a fine fleet. This has had off years, notably 1812. B. has had trouble with a son who wishes to leave the paternal protection. Is fearless except when faced by a hunger strike, the Pankhurst family, and thoughts of Germany. Patronizes a costly social organization known as the Royal Family, or a reception committee for American heiresstocracy, which also dedicates buildings, poses for stamps, post-cards, motion pictures and raises princesses of Wales for magazine articles and crowning purposes. B. is a monitor of English style; wears a monocle, spats, 'i 'at, cane, pipe, awful accent, and never makes his appearance without a cawld bawth. He detests the word "egotism." Is a celebrated humorist, seeing through all jokes but himself. Ambition: 'Ome sweet 'Ome. Recreation: Tea, Week Ends. Address: Hingland. Clubs: Policemen's, Golf, Jockey, and Suffrage. Epitaph: See Emperor William Again.

BURNS, Robert, surnamed "Bobby," a Scotch bard who wrote love poems about his sweetheart. He thus performed two remarkable feats-- making poetry in the Scotch language, and finding a girl in Scotland who was as beautiful as his lines declare.

BUTTERFLY, Madame, a little Japanese lady whose child has remained the same size and age for the past eight years.

BYRON, Lord, an Englishman who swam rivers, was wise enough to get away from the London weather, helped kindle Greek fire, and wrote poems.

CHAPTER C

CAESAR, Julius, school book writer, river crosser, and a great politician who was not born in Ireland. Entered Roman politics as the leader of the Gang. Was active in military affairs. Became a fair general despite his poor service training. Desired to write a book. Began by taking an army and capturing Europe and England. He did not waste his time with Scotland or Ireland. C. made a river famous by crossing it, and finally included Rome in his history of victories. Became popular with the voters, but had trouble with the Senate. Wrote books and paid his debts. Was finally attacked by a few vested-interest senators, and stabbed by a chum. The murderer was caught, but escaped the gallows. C. was honored with one of the finest funeral orations over delivered over a corpse. He was also awarded a few triumphant arches. Publications: Omnes Gallia est divisa in tres parses. Ambition: Rome: Address: Capitol, Rome. Clubs: Gladiators, Vestal. Was also a member of the Society for the Protection of Roman Ruins. Epitaph: Veni, Vidi.

CAIN, one of our ancestors of whom we do not brag.

CANNON, Honorable Joseph G., late of the Speaker's Chair, House of Representatives, Washington, U. S. A. For centuries C. occupied the chair, and tenderly protected poor railroads and trusts from the unkind remarks of congressmen who knew things and him. Was finally retired from the chair by the Democrats, and from Congress by his constituents. Grave: 1912 election. Heir: Champ Clark. Ambition: Those good old trusty days once more. Address: The Far Back Woods. Epitaph: R. I. P.

CANUTE, a king of England who proved the theory that the ocean could wave at him.

CARLOS, Don, a man who does not believe a head is uneasy which wears a crown. Ambition: Royal Palace, Madrid. Address: Northern Spain.

CARMEN, celebrated Spanish flirt. She worked in the government tobacco factory at Seville until a clever writer and a musician rescued her. Went on the stage. Has appeared in most of the cities throughout the world, made love to several singers, and then been killed by a bull fighter after singing her way through five acts.

CARNEGIE, Andrew, or "Andy," or the Laird of Skibo. A fine old American who went about giving away libraries, advice, peace buildings, and advertising armor plate. When a young Scotchman he scotched his three dollars a week and purchased the steel trust. Later retired. Ambition: Universal peace with all dreadnaughts steel trust armored. Also a library in every town. Recreation: Telling young men how to scorn the root of all fortunes. Also receiving university degrees. Address: University commencement platforms, New York City and Scotland.

CARTER, a doctor who wants everybody to have liver trouble.

CARUSO, Enrico, millionaire opera singer, who appeared in the Victor Talking Machine and New York City. Always had a cold or a sore throat, a condition which assisted materially in filling the house. Like all his contemporaries, C. has been sued for divorce and breach of promise, has lost his jewelry, visited zoological gardens, sung for charity, given farewell concerts, and done other things to help his newspaper and box-office reputation.

CASTELLINE, Count Boni Di, a French gold prospector who was successful for a time in the U. S.

CASTOR, one of Leda's twins. Also invented an oil (see Pollux).

CASTRO, Cipriano, of Venezuela. First man to introduce American-Irish politics into South America. Acquired a fortune, which was greatly increased by a personal friendship with the American asphalt trust. Was revolutioned a few times, and finally escaped with the mint and his life. Career: Dangerous. Ambition: Subjects without guns? and a New York police force in his country. Recreation: Taxes. Address: ?

CHAMBERLAIN, Joe A., of England. A former Lloyd-George of the Treasury, who had different ideas of taxation.

CHARON, ferryman. Never had a childhood. Devoted life to his business. Has navigated more people than all the Atlantic liners combined. Ambition: A launch. Recreation: None. Address: The Styx.

CHAUCER (first name unknown), an early experimenter in the English language. Notorious as a bad speller. His best-known work is used as a student puzzle in leading universities and colleges. Ambition: A typewriter and a dictionary.

CHINAMAN, John, a well-known character in the U. S. who washed clothes, and made chop suey until he had enough money to return to his native land, purchase a few wives, and live in opium.

CHURCHILL, Winston, wrote books for a living.

CHURCHILL, Winston, did not write books for a living.

CINCINNATUS, of Rome, who left his plow to make his share in politics. Later inaugurated the back-to-the-farm movement.

CINDERELLA, the only scullion maid who had a small foot and two sisters in society. Historians have questioned her claims to fame, but they may easily be substantiated by millions of children.

CLAUS, Santa, poor father.

CLEOPATRA, of Egypt. A queen who presented England with a threadless needle, fell in love with some foreigners, was unsuccessful in her love and naval affairs, and finally became a mummy through the auspices of an adder. Ambition: An Egyptian St. Patrick. Also Royal lovers. Recreation: Barging with Anthony. Epitaph: Pyramid.

CLIMBERS, T. H. E., an American man and woman who had money and ambition. Spent the early portion of their lives gathering cash, and the later in spending it. Were welcomed by many people, but never quite reached the top. Both died trying to get there. Ambition: An English nobleman in the family. Recreation: Paris, London, and Switzerland. Address: See Recreation. Clubs: All, with the exception of the ones they wanted.

COLE, King, a merry old monarch of the Kingdom of Childhood. Great smoker, and was fond of the bowl. Recreation: Fiddlers.

COLEMAN, a man whose invention has caused tears and throat burnings.

COLUMBUS, Christopher, map enlarger, skipper. Said to have been born in Genoa. Something made him believe the world was round. He endeavored to secure money to prove his theory, but nobody cared whether he was correct or not. Realizing there was no capital or prophet in his own country, he took passage to Spain. There he inveigled Isabella into equipping an expedition for him to discover America. She did and he did. Ambition: To keep New York City in the family. Recreation: Deck shuffle-boards, dreaming. Address: San Salvatore. Clubs: Palos Yacht.

COMPANY, T. H. E., a man and woman who invariably called when we were taking a nap or dressing. Charming conversationalists. Recreation: Tea. Ambition: An invitation to dinner.

CONFUCIUS, A Chinese preacher of note. Lived some 500 years B. C. and taught the chinks the art of joss making, and how to do things backward. He also was the founder of ancestor worship. This still is practiced in England, but never in the United States or Australia. Recreation: Fireworks. Ambition: A Chinese laundry in every city. Epitaph: More Majorum.

CONQUEROR, Will The, of Normandy. Wrote "Hastings" and "1066" in all history books.

COOK, T. H. E., Lord of the Household. Entered the kitchen at a tender age. Soon acquired considerable weight in person, and in the management of the house. When she departed there was weeping, and wailing, and waiting. Diet: Usually large and everything of the best. Ambition: An American policeman, or Thomas Atkins. Recreations: Days off. Address: The whole house.

COOK, Captain, a real explorer who discovered the Sandwich Islands and who took the first Cook's tour around the world.

COOK, Doctor Frederick A., an explorer who said he discovered the north pole, but nobody believed him. (See Peary.)

COOK, Tom, celebrated ticket seller, author of captivating travel literature, and a tour arranger who guarantees to save you money. Owns and operates the Nile and Mount Vesuvius. Publications: The Come On Books. Ambition: Those Americans who want to see everything. Also "first timers." Address: Any foreign city equipped with tourists.

COOK (first name not known), son of the above, who helps his father save money for the tourist. He is called "fils" in Paris.

COPPERFIELD, Dave, one of Dickens' friends who assisted him in building a reputation.

CORBETT, James J., known as "gentleman Jim," one-time champion fighter of the world, and a "has been" for whom everybody has a good word. Many persons wish he might be the Corbett he used to be. Ambition: A white champion.

CORELLI,[1] Marie, an old-maid authoress who wrote delightful love scenes. She is said to have written some books which brought her fame and royalty. C. does not approve of society except her own. She remains secluded with her typewriter at Mason Croft, Stratford-on-Avon, only being seen by her publishers and the editor. Publications: See book stores and railway stations. Recreation: Flowers. Clubs: All anti-suffragette.

---

[1] Ed. Note: The editor hopes to remove this name before the next edition. Its insertion is entirely due to the machinations of book reviewers, who claim Miss Corelli's books have fallen into the "was" class. The editor never contradicts a book reviewer.

COXEY, General, leader of the only non-militant army in the world which did not take up collections or give away Christmas dinners.

CRITIC, Dramatic, a notorious prevaricator who tells the world to see all the shows, and thus preserves the advertising column for his employers.

CROESUS, an ancient John D. Rockefeller, who became wealthy without trusts, the Supreme Court, or the stock market.

CROKER, Dick, ex-king of New York City. Born in Ireland of Irish parents. From childhood he practiced the art of politics, which resulted in his gaining the friendship of the New York police force. C. was elected. C. was very poor. Later retired to his native land with two Atlantic liners filled with salary. Ambition: An Irish president. Recreation: English Derbys. Address: Ireland. Clubs: 1,100,000 New York Democratic.

CROMWELL, Oliver, a militant Presbyterian who entered politics, and went about England tearing down churches. He also assisted in putting King Charles I. out of his pleasure. Ran things in England on a reform-Cromwell basis, and after his death was honored by having his round head placed as a decoration over Westminster Hall.

CRUSOE, Robinson, F. R. G. S., traveller and autobiographer. Visited a sparsely-settled island in the Pacific Ocean; talked to parrots; found some footprints; rescued Friday, and returned to England to become an author.

CUPID, Daniel, a cute little fat fellow who called on every one at least once. Born shortly after Adam, and is still up to mischievous tricks. It was he who made kings fall in love with poor country girls; chauffeurs with their ladies, and beggars with princesses. C. held all men and women equal provided they were good, and he made the happiest people on earth when they listened to his voice. He witnessed several international engagements, but did not like them, as the contestants gave him a black eye. He also was responsible for mothers-in-law. Some roads he made very rough, but C. always was a good guide. At times he caused pain, but he said it never was his fault. When C. stayed in a house the sun was always shining. You should be at home when he calls. Ambition: That sigh. Recreation: Archery. Address: Perhaps you know. Clubs: None. He prefers the fireside and moonlight nights.

CURIE, Madame, one of the few women who got her name in print without being a suffragette or an actress.

CZAR. See Russia.

CHAPTER D

DANIEL, ancient lion tamer. Also performed the difficult feat of remaining in a fiery furnace without his family applying for the insurance.

DANTE, of Italy, architect of the under world, journalist, lover, and poor politician. Wrote articles for magazines, but used too much slang. Later fell in love. The girl (see her) knew what journalists were, and refused to spoon. Exasperated, he began a bombardment of poetry. That settled it. D. then entered politics. Soon learned they did not mix with love and his business. Both he and his manuscripts were banished. Traveled in Italy in the interests of safety. Posed for his bust while suffering with a bad attack of dyspepsia. Publications: Poems, tragedies, and comedies (?). Ambition: To be Beatrice's Romeo. Recreation: Travel. Address: II via Dante, Florence. Seldom at home.

DANTON, the man who wound up France before the revolution.

DARLING, Grace, a light-house keeper's daughter who showed the world that a woman may fear a mouse, but not a tempest. One of the truly brave who did not receive a Carnegie advertisement.

DARWIN, Charlie, a well-known enemy of preachers. He discovered that many men looked like their progenitors, and proved his theories with the exception of one link. The clergymen claimed that a chain with one link missing was no chain, and that D. was a nature faker. Publications: Origin of

Species, a valuable book, even if it does fail to explain the currency bill.

DAUGHTER, Pharaoh's, an Egyptian princess, who took a bath, and rescued little Moses from the bull rushes. (See Mose.)

DAVID, King, or "Dave," shepherd, writer, musician, champion sling shot, and politician. Son of poor parents. Entered army as a volunteer, and was awarded medals for his attack upon Goliath. Appointed musician to the royal household. Became friendly with the Prince of Wales and succeeded in doing him out of the coronation. Later was elected king. Fell in love with Mrs. (name not mentioned by newspapers). Gave her husband a conspicuous position in the army. Married her. Heir: Sol. Publications: Psalms. Recreation: Slinging. Address: Jerusalem.

DEATH, a hideous man who called at least once during a lifetime, usually toward the close. Patron of insurance companies. Nothing is known of his childhood. Historians claim he never had any. Possessed an ugly face; wore a sheet over his head, and always carried a scythe in his hands. Never brought happiness, although his visits frequently gave money to some one. Never could be bribed to pass a house he wished to enter. Many doctors and scientists have endeavored to kill him, but he continues to be a safe bet at 100 to 1. Heir: None. Ambition: A happy home and prosperous graveyards. Recreation: Sharpening scythes. Address: Always hung out a black cloth wherever he resided.

DELILAH, friend of Samson, and quite a dip. She also accompanied Samson on a number of European and American opera expeditions.

DELMONICO, founder of a Fifth Avenue New York City cafe, where the cost of living has ever been high. He introduced the French menu into the U. S. and with it considerable indigestion.

DEMOSTHENES, an old Greek talker.

DENIS, Saint, a saint with an Irish name who made good in France.

DEPEW, Chauncey M., an ancient railroad-wealthy U. S. Senator from the state of New York. He made after-dinner speeches, dedicated monuments; married a young wife, and was relegated to obscurity by the American voters.

DESDEMONA, of Venice. A lady whose handkerchiefs cost more than her clothes.

DESLYS, G., a French dancer who had sufficient charm to attract a royal press agent, who could draw crowds and a big salary.

DEVIL, see Old Nic.

DEWAR, John, inventor of a popular Scotch beverage without which no cold day is complete.

DEWEY, George E., a former American hero who totally destroyed a Spanish armada in Manila Bay. He received the homage of a nation; had cigars named after him; appeared in Who's Who; was paraded through the streets; married a widow; moved to Washington; got in bad with the inhabitants, and got out of the newspapers.

DIANA, an ancient sportswoman who loved fox hunting, hounds, and the chase without the conventionalities of a society hunt. Address: Ephesus.

DIAZ, Porfiro, former king and political leader of Mexico, who departed from the social functions of a king to assist the government. Legends prevail to the effect that he patterned his actions on a Napoleon-Roosevelt policy. He also was requested to move. Ambition: A revolution with himself on top. Recreation: The fandango. Address: Fifty years in the White House of Mexico. Epitaph: Wilson Never Bothered Me.

DICE, see Thomas and Harry.

DICE, Diamond, American ten-cent adventurer; friend of the messenger boys and embryo criminals. His biography formed an important part in the lives of the boys who never visited the Carnegie libraries.

DICKENS, Charles, an English writer who wrote.

DIN, Gunga, a limpin' lump of brick dust, water carrier. Employed in H. R. H. service in India. Wore few clothes. Fought in many battles. Frequently gave bad water to soldiers. Rescued Thomas Atkins, but was shot while in the act. Saved the government the price of a medal. His pathetic story was widely published. Later it fell into disfavor in the U. S. and Great Britain, it now being considered a crime to recite the story. Ambition: To come back like Sherlock Holmes. Recreation: Sleep. Address: Care of biographer.

DIOGENES, the most foolish man who ever lived. He endeavored to find something with a lantern which could not even be located with a searchlight. Ambition: A brighter lantern.

Recreation: Cleaning globes. Address: Tub. Epitaph: Here Lies A Man Who Attempted The Impossible.

DISRAELI, a Hebrew who gave up the trades of his ancestors to run England.

DOE, John, an honest man who was defrauded out of millions by persons who forged his name.

DOODLE, Yankee, American horseman who made people take off their hats, shout, and whistle when he rode into town.

DORCAS, a modiste who founded the church gossip societies.

DOWIE, alias Elijah II, a celebrated Chicago divine who showed the world how easily some people were deprived of their money and religion.

DRAKE, Francis, an English admiral who did not have a public square named after him. D. also introduced the spud into Ireland.

DREAMER, T. H. E., castle builder. Lived long ago, and intended doing something to-day. Spent much time thinking about the best girl in the world. A great friend of Procrastinator. Went through life waiting for to-morrow. Several men, however, with the same name, have awakened and given their dreams to the world (see Columbus, etc., and Lady Macbeth).

DREW, John, prehistoric American actor.

DREYFUS, Captain, founder of the Dreyfus Case. Got out of jail by being one of the few innocent men who got into print.

DUFF, Mac, a Scotchman who gained fame because he was a good layer on.

DUMPTY, H., celebrated accident victim. Fell from a wall at an early age and never recovered, despite the services of specialists.

DUN, another man whose word of commendation will enable you to open a charge account.

CHAPTER E

EASTMAN, George, inventor of the brownie camera and the most expensive sport on earth. Ambition: The kodak fiend, tourists. Address: Rochester and London. Clubs: Camera.

EDDY, Mrs., of Boston, Mass., U. S. A., a lady who made millions by telling the world there was no such thing as the toothache, sea-sickness, or hitting your thumb with a hammer.

EDISON, Thomas, an American who invented everything with the exception of the sun dial, Pear's soap, and the Gillette razor.

EIFEL, a Frenchman who built the second tower of Babel, but who was wise enough to stop before he got too high.

EIGHTH, Henry the, suitor, blue beard, and church builder. When a young man he became a benedict, a condition in which he remained until well along in years. As fast as a queen appeared at the breakfast table with her hair down her back, she was dispatched to the block. A couple of queens got ahead of him. Was nearly as successful in obtaining divorces as Napoleon, of France, and American millionaires. In his later years he competed against the Pope in England. Ambition: A harem. Recreation: Spooning. Dreams: Bad. Address: Windsor.

ELGIN, Lord, the man who rolled the Elgin marbles from Greece to the British Museum. Also had something to do with the interior of watches.

ELIJAH, a prophet of old who was fond of ravens (not red). Later he went somewhat out of his line, but succeeded as a chariot driver.

ELIZABETH, Queen, called "Bess" by Raleigh and the rest of the boys. E. reigned when people did things. She was wooed and lost by an Armada (see Philip II). She finally walked over Raleigh's coat, and later wiped her feet on him. E. had a sister by the name of Mary, who was better looking, and less fortunate. E. was queen when the pipe was introduced into England. Other and less important events of her reign were: Shakespeare, Spenser, and Virginia. Died an old maid. Heir: She did not have any.

ELLIOT, George, a lady who wore a man's name and wrote books.

EMANUEL II, Victor, the original of the statues in every town of Italy; a king with ambitions, who was wise enough to entrust his affairs to a brainier man, and was thus made famous (see Girabaldi).

EMERSON, Ralph Waldo, American writer who inspired his readers to conquer the world. Several have failed. Also advised the practical theory of hitching your wagon to the stars. Lived before the time of the taxi.

EPICURUS, an ancient who believed that pain was unpleasant and that pleasure was good. His descendants live in expensive hotels and eat only in high-class restaurants. Many suffer with the gout. A popular cat foot was named in his honor.

ESAU, an ancient who sold his birthright for a mess of breakfast food.

ESTHER, Queen, a beautiful lady who triumphed over the villain of the book, married the hero, and lived happily ever afterward.

EUCLID, an old Greek who made poor students read his book as far back as 300 B. C. He discovered the phenomenon that the shortest distance between two points is a crow's flight, and that two parallel lines always compete.

EVE, see Mrs. Adam.

EYRE, Jane, an old maid school teacher, who married a rich husband after the fashion of books.

CHAPTER F

FAGAN, the Hebrew benefactor of Oliver Twist, whose name did not fit his religion.

FAHRENHEIT, inventor of an instrument which enables a person to ascertain whether the weather is warm or cold.

FAILURE, T. H. E., a failure. Supposed to have idled away his younger days. Believed to have dissipated. Said not to have applied himself to school or business. Found fault with life and everybody, but was never wrong himself. Unpopular. A great blamer. A lover of revolvers, rivers, and the poor house. Frequently seen in the under world. Ambition: The other fellow. Recreation: Too much. Address: All large cities. Clubs: None. Epitaph: Here Lies A Man Who Never Really Tried.

FALLIERES, Armand, occupied a prominent position in the French government for seven years. One of the most distinguished of the vast collection of ex-presidents now scattered over the world.

FALSTAFF, a celebrated drunk.

FASHION, Dame, heart breaker, bank account ruiner, and patron saint of French shop-keepers. She went about the large stores changing the cut of ladies' clothes and the shape of their hats. Created some awful looking things. F. made the poor men work very hard to keep up to her. Publications: Editor of all Ladies' Magazines. Address: Paris, London, and New York City. Epitaph: (Would that she had one.)

FAUST, chemist, traveler. A gay old man who fell in love during his second young manhood, traveled in a warm country, and sang his way to fame.

FAWES, Guy, a man who attempted to make an impression in Parliament without introducing home rule or suffrage bills.

FINN, Huc, a bosom friend of Thomas Sawyer (see Tom).

FITZIMMONS, Robert, an obsolete fighter who wishes he could rub the black spot from the ring.

FLETCHER, the inventor of chewing.

FLORADORA, an American chorus girl, who was some popular with the men. She appeared in all large cities with the best looking chorus that ever wore tights. F. created such a sensation that every living actress of note is willing to be classified as a former member of her company. Had a miserable cigar named after her. Ambition: Revival. Grave: New York City. Epitaph: There Were Not Many Like Flora.

FOGG, P., The man Jules Verne sent around the world in sixty days for a big sale.

FOOL, A., a spendthrift lover. Fell in love with an unintelligent woman and one who never could understand. Followed his natural bents, even as you and I. Wasted several years. Wept profusely. End unknown. Recreation: Vampires. Epitaph: He Was Not The Only One.

FRANKLIN, Benjamin, one of the few Americans endowed with brains. He discovered that lightning was composed of electricity, that politics paid better than printing, and that the French Court was more lively than the Continental Congress.

FRERES, Pathe, patron of the motion picture fanatics.

FRIEND, A., the scarcest thing on earth. A rare visitor, but he came around a few times in a lifetime. F. was glad to know of your success, pitied you in your failures, and shook you by the hand when you were down and out. Never borrowed money, but he frequently lent it. Was a wise counsellor. Very popular. His name was frequently given the baby (see Mischief). Ambition: The other fellow's welfare. Recreation: At the other fellow's house. Address: The other fellow's house or his own. Clubs: All.

FRITCHIE, Barbara, a Southern target. Sprang into poetry as the only woman in the history of mankind who admitted her old age.

FULTON, Robert, inventor. Another brainy American who made a fortune for the Cunard and White Star lines.

CHAPTER G

GABRIEL, A., trumpeter. Entered history at an early date as the agent for the Garden of Eden. Compelled the Adam family to move. Historians claim he will again be in Who's Who when St. Peter (see him) makes the inventory. Ambition: Larger lungs. Recreation: Aviation.

GAINSBOROUGH, T. R. A., a versatile English hat and portrait manufacturer.

GALILEO, inventor, star gazer. Proved himself an imbecile by declaring the world revolved when everybody knew it was stationary. Manufactured the first spy-glass, an instrument which has since been used in theatres and for various other purposes. Also discovered that clocks were equipped with pendulums.

GANGSTER, T. H. E., a politician known as a "progressive" when out of office.

GARDEN, Mary, a clever actress who succeeded on the opera stage. Legend has it that Mary possessed a fine voice as a child. This was expensively cultivated in Europe, was later exposed before English and American congregations, and her Sapho-Salome-Thais-Carmen costumes packed the houses. Ambition: Less wealth and more throat. She also wants a husband with a soul. Recreation: Being presented with opera houses and suppers. Residence: Principally Atlantic liners.

GARIBALDI, G., the George Washington of Italy without the tea party. He espoused the cause of Victor Emmanuel (see Victor), and successfully Bismarcked the Italian States. Slept in every town in his country, ran second to V. E. in the number of statues erected to his appearance, and for three years held the championship for eating spaghetti.[1]

GARRICK, an old English matinee idol.

GATLING, R. J., he was considered a big gun.

GAUL, Dying, a brave soldier who posed for his statue when mortally wounded.

GEORGE I, King of England, 1660-1727. Permitted the whigs in general, and one Walpole in particular, to run England.

GEORGE II, King of England, 1683-1760. Held a few wars.

GEORGE III, King of England, 1736-1820. Lived during the reign of William Pitt, and believed in taxing tea.

GEORGE IV, husband of Queen Mary (see front pages of our contemporary Who's Who).

GEORGE-LLOYD, Dave, a well-known cigar, English politician. Entered politics via a newspaper, clever speeches, and votes. Was a modest member of the House of Commons, seldom speaking more than four times on any bill. Kept climbing until he became under secretary of something, order keeper of the Board of Trade, and finally occupied a prominent position in the Exchequer. Assisted the Primer to grasp the Irish home rule

---

[1] Ed. Note: This is not an advertisement.

millstone, and hung on without a gurgle. Ambition: A dynamite-proof house, a tax on air. Recreation: (see Asquith). Address: Front row House of Commons. Clubs: Anti-conservative.

GIBSON, Charles Dana, American artist who pleased the old inhabitants before the market was so wet.

GILLETTE, manufacturer of a well-known Christmas present which cuts barbers out of their tips, and is deucedly annoying to clean.

GIRL, The Chorus, Um!

GLADIATOR, Dying, another brave artists' model.

GLADSTONE, W. E., a grand old man who twice premiered England, chopped trees, and failed to make accurate measurements with the Irish home rule.

GLYNN, E., an old maid authoress who knew things. Wrote a book which everybody tells the rector they have not read, and then re-reads it when the doors are locked. In the United States a law has been passed compelling booksellers to include a bottle of disinfectant whenever a G. book is sold. Ambition: A publisher who is not afraid of the police. Recreation: Reading her own books. Address: Probably Paris. Clubs: Always blackballed.

GOAT, T. H. E., the one who purchased this book.

GODIVA, Lady, horsewoman whose costume rivalled many exhibited at the Paris horseshow. Many said her habit was out of sight.

GOETHE, a Dutchman who succeeded in making a few German words rhyme.

GOLIATH, ancient heavyweight champion, who was knocked out in one round by a lightweight. Defeat attributed to overconfidence. Friends said nothing like that had ever entered his head.

GOODWIN, Nathaniel, an American who was opposed to Mormonism, but who adopted it on a progressive and newspaper scale.

GOOSE, Mother, a fine old lady who was loved by all, but who told some awful untruths to the innocent.

GORDON, I. L., editor of Who Was Who. Probably the greatest writer who ever lived. Spent early childhood in infancy. At the age of fourteen began shaving and wearing long trousers. At twenty-one G. was considered of age. Began writing while a child. Penmanship so poor he took to the typewriter. Wrote Who Was Who with hope someone would purchase it. Some one did. Ambition: (He considers this personal and will not be quoted.) Recreation: Looking for publishers. Address: Paris when financially able. Other times in one of those confounded newspaper offices.

GORKY, M., a resident of Russia who became unpopular with the government and moved. He endeavored to make a lecture tour of the United States accompanied by another man's wife. Learned that this was not the usual custom in America. His managers and hotel proprietors requested him to continue his travels. Ambition: A czarless Russia; less fussy people. Publications: Much unpatriotic literature.

GRAY, the man who wrote a clever cemetery poem, the first line of which is remembered by everybody.

GREAT, Peter the, shipbuilder, and the only ruler of Russia who never was bombarded. Was also unique in the fact that he worked. Historians claim this was due to his poor salary.

GROAT, John, proprietor of a celebrated house located some distance from Land's End.

GUILLOTIN, Doctor, a French inventor of a popular method of decapitation, who had such confidence in his invention that he was the first to give it a practical demonstration.

GULLIVER, a Munchausen-Doctor Cook-Peary traveler who never submitted his proofs, but who found a credulous publisher and a gullible public. Never lectured.

CHAPTER H

HAFID, Mulai, a sultan of Morocco, who succeeded in abdicating before he was abdicated.

HAGAR, Miss, Abraham's wife's maid who nearly broke up a happy family.

HAHNEMANN, Doctor, of Leipsig, discovered the sugar pill and called it homeopathy.

HAM, second officer and engineer of the Ark.

HAMED, Abdul, a retired professor of diplomacy, champion promiser, and a sick man. When a youth he began instructing the monarchs of Europe in the use of a government. One of his favorite pastimes was reading ultimatums. Fearless until a warship entered the harbor, and even then usually got rid of it with promises. Employed massacres to break the monotony of reigning. Acquired as fine a harem as ever sat on silk cushions. Some of H.'s younger subjects though he should be ostlerized (see Dr. Ostler). They gave him his harem and salary, and locked him up in a palace. Then the wise ones lost Tripoli and about everything but sleeping room in Europe. Motto: I told you so. Ambition: To be back on the job. Recreations: Private entertainments. Address: Harem. Epitaph: Everybody Worked But Father.

HAMLET, a Dane who had difficulty with an auxiliary verb. Also founded the foolish questions.

HAMMERSTEIN, Oscar, an opera broker who inflicted himself, high prices, and buildings upon certain communities.

HANDEL, placed "Handel's Largo" on the music stands. Also wrote a few other airs.

HARRY. (See Thomas and Richard.)

HARVARD, John, an Englishman who founded a great American university near the cultured town of Boston, Mass., U. S. A., where football players and the sons of American millionaires eke out an education.

HARVEY, Doctor W., a physician who learned in 1619 that his patients had blood which circulated. The discovery has since been of some profit to his successors.

HEINZ, of Pittsburg, Pa. A man who never tried to conceal his name. Sold American baked beans, catsup, and fifty-five other varieties to the world.

HELENA, Saint, Constantine's mother. She built a few churches (also see Napoleon).

HEMANS, Mrs., poetess who gave to the world that rich, soulful, and exquisite poesy, "The Boy Stood on the Burning Deck." It is said the poem has been parodized.

HENRY, Pat., an Irish-American politician who demanded liberty or death. From all that can be ascertained he secured the latter.

HERCULES, the Sandow of the ancients, promoter of the Olympic games and laborer. H. claimed to have done some things which are even questioned by the partisans of Doctor

Cook. Killed about everybody, erected two pillars, stole some apples, and, in short, did everything but enter politics or invent a breakfast food. Ambition: The thirteenth labor. Recreation: Muscle development, travel. Address: The Pillars. Clubs: Athletic. Epitaph: Now Is A Mighty Man Fallen.

HIAWATHA, American Indian who permitted his wife to starve to death simply for the want of proper nourishment. Many claim a great American poet used bad taste in writing the biography of such a man.

HICHENS,[1] Robert, planter of the Garden of Allah. Experimented with belle donna. H. is still in Who's Who, and multitudes of readers hope he will remain there for some time to come. Ambition: Sales. Recreation: Filling his fountain pen or cleaning typewriter. Address: Care of the Publisher. Home: Sicily.

HILL, Samuel, a man who did things in a hurry. Also a celebrated rain storm.

HOBSON, American-Spanish War hero who lowered his ideals and went to Congress. Later he became a temperance lecturer. Was heard by great crowds. Produced statistics to show how few saloons failed after a lecture.

HOLMES, Sherlock, detective. When a child he devoured inexpensive literature and theatres. This fired his mind to eliminate Scotland Yard as a crime-detecting agency. Entered the profession of a detective, but was unknown until Doctor Watson pulled him into print. His fortune was then made. All the society scandals were placed in his hands, and if he only told what he knew about society--! H. solved the most complicated

---

[1] Ed. Note: The editor hopes to meet Mr. Hichens some day, and is compelled to make the biography flattering.

mysteries with a stroke of his hypodermic needle, and was only baffled in locating the murderer of Cock Robin. His name struck terror into the hearts of criminals and competing publishers. After all the criminals in England had been jailed or hung he was killed by an author, but the great H. solved the mystery of the grave and came back to life in time to see his murderer knighted. Now at work on the suffragette case. Ambition: Another Dr. Watson. Recreation: Fond of Doyle's works and the violin. Address: 31 Baker Street. Clubs: London Prison Society. Epitaph: Au Revoir, But.

HOMER, travel writer, mythology expert, and journalist. Began career as a reporter on the Athens "Times." Was discharged for incompetence, and took up honest writing. Found a publisher who thought his writings would sell to posterity. Later H. took charge of the Ulysses Tours. Was war correspondent for the Greek associated press at the siege of Troy. Ambition: Fewer classics and more money. Publication: See libraries and school rooms. Address: Care Athens. Clubs: Literary, Fourth Estate.

HOOD, Red Riding, a brave little girl who escaped alive from a wolf which had previously partaken of a relative.

HOOD, Robin, a fine robber of merry England who took from the rich and gave to the poor, and made crackerjack material for stories.

HOOD, Sarsaparilla, the manufacturer of another remedy for Harvey's discovery.

HOPE, the most beautiful woman who ever lived. She was a near relation of Ambition. Discovered the words "wish" and "if" and gave her name to the world. She was the first woman to manufacture ideals, and has been made the patron saint of the suffragettes (see Suffragette). H. went about making life worth while. She was loved by all those millions of lovers and all those millions of men and women who endeavored to do things. Ambition: The discouraged. Recreation: Success. Address: Perhaps she has resided in your home.

HORACE, Quintus Horatius Flaccus, a rhymester of Greece who sang and drank of the Falernian wine.

HORATIUS, Roman bridge tender who saved the city, and swam the Tiber without getting stuck in the mud.

HOUR, The Man of the, most popular and versatile man who ever lived. Attracted tremendous attention. Newspapers printed his picture and ran long articles about his life, family, eccentricities, etc. Won fame in war, science, pulpit, aviation, stage, art, music, politics, literature, finance, by saving a life and in exploring. His accomplishments were infinite. H. was lionized by royalty, society, and beautiful women. Made addresses, gave interviews, received honors. He was the man everyone wanted to shake by the hand so they could tell other people they had done it. Ambition: Another hour. Recreation: Basking. Address: All countries. Clubs: All open.

HUERTA, Victoriano, a Mexican who made it necessary to employ extra telegraphers and throat lotions at the White House. He also was responsible for the phrase, "The Mexican Situation."

HUR, Benjamin, chariot racer, actor. Appeared in all large cities, showed his noble figure, raced his horses, downed the villain, packed up, and moved to the next town.

HURST, William Randolph, father of the American unwhitened newspapers. Democrat. Started life in a humble manner, only controlling a few newspapers. He soon purchased others. His magical touch changed their color. Employed the greatest staff of imaginary geniuses ever gathered together. These men had the ability to write unhampered by mere details or facts. H. also employed many good lawyers and used them frequently. Fortified by his constituents, to wit: the aforesaid geniuses and newspapers, H. entered politics as a candidate for anything. Was always Bryaned and Roosevelted. Ambition: Same as Bryan. Recreation: Reading yellow journals. Address: All large American cities. Epitaph: The Vote Is Mightier Than The Pen.

HYDE, Mr. (See Dr. Jekyll.)

CHAPTER I

IBYCUS, a Grecian poet who improved poetry by permitting words to rhyme at the ends of the lines.

ICARUS, father of aviation. Record holder for the first tumble. Selected water as the spot for his fall, and was not picked up with the debris. Ambition: A Wright machine. Recreation: Tuning up. Address: Greece. Clubs: Aero.

IEKATERINOGRADSK, of Russia. Little is known of his life except that he built a celebrated fort to protect the poor Cossacks from the molestations of the populace. Was probably blown up or died in prison.

INGERSOLL, first man to bring the price of turnips to within the reach of authors and artists. Historians claim he would have made another fortune had he lived when the sun-dial trust had its own way.

INGERSOLL, Robt. G., one of those contented souls who did not believe in anything, and made a fortune by telling people what he believed.

INNOCENT, thirteen popes. Address: Rome.

IRVING, Washington, a pleasing American writer who visited Westminster Abbey, made Rip Van Winkle wake up, and wrote a few biographies.

ISAAC (last name unknown), s. Abraham and Sarah.[1] Spent his childhood like all little Isaacs and later married Rebecca, claimed by historians to have been a Jewess. Had two famous sons, Esau and Jake (see both, but especially the latter). Died at the tender age of 180 years.

ISABELLA, a Spanish queen who vowed she would not change her clothes until the Moors were driven from the country. Her husband, the king, raised an army and accomplished the feat. I.'s name is sometimes connected with the discovery of America. This, however, is an error, as Columbus took a more active part.

ISAIAH, a prophet who wore second-hand clothing.

ISHMAEL, son of Abraham, whose appearance complicated his father's estate. Traveled extensively in the desert with his mother.

---

[1] Ed. Note: The editor apologizes for a seeming familiarity He did his best to ascertain the lady's last name, but failed.

CHAPTER J

JACK, the man who kept company with Jill. Occupation: Water carrier. Killed while at work. Ambition: An artesian well in the valley. (See Jill.)

JACOB, birthright speculator, traveler, s. Isaac, and brother of Esau. Was mother's pet. Became proficient as a character impersonator, but never went on the stage. Left home suddenly. Slept on a stone and had hard dreams. Later married, and was responsible for Joseph and his brethren. (See Joe.)

JAEGER, Doctor Gustav, claimed his underwear kept him warm.

JAMES, Jesse, an American westerner who murdered, stole, and appeared in paper novels for the benefit of the messenger boy, the author, and the publisher.

JAMES, King, a Scotchman who was considered good enough to be elected king of England.

JANOS, H., manufacturer of a popular beverage.

JAPHETH, third officer of the Ark.

JEFFERSON, Joe, a fine old memory.

JEFFREYS, James J., formerly a prize fighter, who carried his gloves and bluff once too often to the ring. (See Johnson.)

JEKYLL, Doctor, a physician who took a dose of his own medicine.

JEW, Wandering, an ancient Hebrew who has been going over the face of the earth for centuries, only stopping at the call of such men as Eugene Sue and Lew Wallace.

JILL, Jack's girl. She was assisting her fiance when the accident occurred.

JOB, prehistoric millionaire who had his ups and downs. Like all rich men, he had a good young manhood, saved his money, and entered the market. Formed the camel trust and cornered the real estate market. The market tumbled and so did J. Family troubles also distressed him. His camels died of the colic or were stolen. J. went broke. Even in hard luck he patronized the temple, and believed while there was money it could be had. Started in business again with a small capital, remarried, and ended his days ahead of the game. Ambition: A chance at the New York Stock market; death to his comforters. Recreation: Sackcloth and ashes.

JOHNSON, John, called "Jack," one-time black champion prize-fighter of the world, who learned that too much chicken, automobile, and champagne made even a colored gentleman a "waser."

JOHNSON, Samuel, no relation of the above. Employed the greatest press agent the world has ever seen, and was thus made famous. Also wrote.

JONAH, traveler, whaler, and lucky dog. Became renowned for taking a rough trip to sea. Was thrown overboard because he was the jonah. Swam until he was tired, and finally made a morsel for a fish. Tradition has it that J. was tough and indigestible. He remained three days and three nights in the interior of the whale, causing the animal considerable annoyance when he exercised. Was later mal de mared, swam ashore, and thanked his lucky stars for his indigestibility and the illness of his rescuer. His story was published. Still causes some comment. Tradition also says that J. never could look a fish in the face after the harrowing incident. Ambition: Dry land. Recreation: Mountain climbing. Address: Sodom. Clubs: Alpine.

JONATHAN, a man who loved King David more than a successor.

JONES, John, made a fortune for Europe by inventing the picture post-card.

JONES, John Paul, an American admiral who scared England, and was only prevented from capturing London by the unimportance of the place.

JOSEPH, a Hebrew-Egyptian politician. Born in Judea. When a young man he became his father's favorite, while his brethren had to do the heavy work. Wore a loud coat. This aroused the ire of his brethren, resulting in Joe being sold as a slave, and in the coat being sent to the cleaners. J. journeyed to Egypt, where he refused to elope with the Pharaohess. Her husband, the Pharaoh, out of gratitude, put J. in prison, and afterward made him the royal butler. Years passed. A famine occurred in Judea. Joe's brethren came down to Egypt to lay in provisions. There they were confronted by the coatless Joe, who thanked them for the good luck they had thrust upon him.

JOSEPHINE, only one of that great multitude of women who carried a heart which was broken by the ambitions of a man.

JUDAS, suicide.

JUDY, Mrs. Punch, but usually unconventionally called by her first name. She suffered considerable annoyance at the hands of her husband, although she frequently hen-pecked him. Went on the puppet stage for a few hundred years, displaying her domestic infelicity.

JULIET, a celebrated sweetheart who permitted her lover to make love on a balcony. Her history was written by one Shakespeare, and had a splendid sale. (See Romeo.)

JUPITER, boss of the ancient gods, father of most of them, and a regular Frenchman. Ambition: To run everything. Recreation: Killing giants, disguising himself as a swan, etc. Address: Olympia.

JUSTICE, only a mythological character whose statue has been frequently erected. She had eye trouble. In the United States J. carried scales with a small statue of politics in one pan, and money in the other. Her statues in other countries are said to be different, although occasionally the little statues are found in the pans.

CHAPTER K

KAISER, T. H. E., alias Emperor William, "Bill" to his friends; a German of some prominence, who caused heartfailure in Europe, considerable comment in England, and much applause in his own country. Was also a naval constructor. Born of royal parents. Inherited his father's position. At a tender age he formed a passion for an army. Like all royal children, he had his own way. His plaything has grown steadily, is in fine condition, but is only used for parading and scaring purposes. His later years were spent in making additions to the fleet, but for what purpose even the wisest sages could not guess. K. was also honored by a visit from T. Roosevelt (see the Wonder) on his exhibition through Europe. It is said he could not learn anything from his adviser. Heir: The crown prince. Ambition: His army applied to the socialists. Recreation: Army. Address: Army. Clubs: Army.

KEELEY, Doctor, water-wagon manufacturer. Claimed fame solely on account of the invention which prevented men from going home to a scolding without the assistance of lamp posts. Declared his cure was as good as gold. Was strongly opposed by John Barleycorn and his friends. Never cared for New York, London, or Paris. K.'s end never has been made public. Historians are endeavoring to ascertain whether he practiced what he preached. Ambition: Large breweries. Recreation: Getting away from business. Address: All large cities. Clubs: W. C. T. U.

KHAYYAM, Omar, a fine old Persian who wrote a beautiful and heartfelt commentary on headache producers. Ambition: More grapes. Recreation: A flask, books, and a Persian "thou." Epitaph: He Certainly Practised What He Preached.

KIDD, Captain, the man who spent his life burying the treasure which several people have been sure they could locate. Was said to have been one of the finest men who ever scuttled a ship.

KILLER, Jack The Giant, a man who combined his name and accomplishments.

KIPLING, Rudyard, an English writer who has not been knighted.

KNOX, John, of Edinburgh. He was the man who introduced the kirk into Scotland, but failed to launch the collection plate.

KRUGER, Oom Paul, an Old Dutch cleanser who certainly made England scrub up.

KUBELIK, Jan, the only violinist who never gave a farewell concert.

CHAPTER L

LACHAISE, Pere, confessor of Louis XIV for thirty-four years. He was such an attentive listener and heard so much that the leading cemetery in Paris was named in his honor.

LAMB, Charles, one of those immortals who forgot his life of tears to place smiles on paper.

LANGTRY, Mrs., the Sarah Bernhardt of England less considerable talent. Ambition: Those old time lovers.

LAOCOON, a Trojan priest who suffered with delirium tremens. Together with his sons he posed for his statue while encumbered with a bad attack. Address: Vatican, Rome.

LAURIE, Annie, of Maxwelton. The only woman in history who had a brow like a snowdrift. Also the only good-looking lassie in Scotland to whom Burns did not write a few poems. L. was engaged to be married; no record of the ceremony can be found.

LAW, Andres Bonar, a Scotchman who gave up the iron business to become a mere member of Parliament. Is said to have spoken on Irish questions. Ambition: (?). Recreation: Travel, except in the south of Ireland. Address: Parliament. This will probably hold good for several editions of Who Was Who. Clubs: Conservative, of course.

LAW,[1] Mother-in-, no relation of the above. A much-abused ancient whose life and story has been written by malicious biographers. In reality L. was a kind soul who invited us to dinner, permitted the gas to be turned down, and always knocked before she came into the room. Later she wiped the dishes, took care of her grandchild (see Baby), helped pay the bills, and told the neighbors what a fine son-in-law she had. Ambition: Daughter. Recreation: Our house. Address: Our house most of the time. Clubs: Suffrage.

LAWSON, Thomas W., just a squeeler.

LEDA, see mythology books, paintings, and statuary. Also Jupiter, Castor, and Pollux.

LEE and PERKINS, discoverers of Worcestershire sauce and royal saucerers to the king.

LEHAR, Frank, the man who assisted the Merry Widow to make her debut. Also was the press agent for Mr. Maxim, of Paris. Ambition: To find another widow.

LEONORE, became famous because she had a lover who left her with a good song.

LEOPOLD, King, of the Congo and Belgium. Has not been dead long enough for historians to make him famous. Ambition: Song, women, and wine. Recreation: Wine, women, and song. Address: Several in Brussels. Epitaph: Quantum Mutatus Ab Illo.

LIBERTY, a huge lady who guards New York harbor, and welcomes Italy and Poland to the United States.

---

[1] Ed. Note: The editor will not be held responsible for the accuracy of the above.

LIMBURGER, of Germany. Manufacturer of a self-advertising cheese.

LIPTON, Sir Thomas, a knighted Irishman who advertised tea with Shamrocks, and one of the men of his race who did not enter politics or the police force. Ambition: That cup.

LISZT, Frank, a piano player who wore long hair, wrote music, and played the piano.

LLOYD, the man who will insure anything except the prospects for the sale of this book.

LORELEI, said to be a beautiful German lady who always hides herself when the tourist goes down the Rhine.

LOT, Mrs. Lot's husband.

LOT, Mrs., the only woman who had an inquisitiveness which became practical. She also was considered one of the salt of the earth.

LOUIS I, 778-840, called the Debonnaire. Introduced cafe's into France. Put the "is" in Paris.

LOUIS II, 846-879. Introduced chorus girls into France. Patron of cafe's.

LOUIS III, 882-936. Introduced champagne into France. Continued the works of his predecessors.

LOUIS IV, 936-954. Introduced high heels. Continued the work of his predecessors.

LOUIS V, 966-987. Introduced absinthe.

LOUIS VI, 1106-1137. Enlarged the works of his ancestors. Started pre-tango dancing.

LOUIS VII, 1137-1180. Fought Germany. Inaugurated the French menu.

LOUIS VIII, 1187-1196. Introduced the words "a la" and dressmakers into Paris.

LOUIS IX, called the saint, 1215-1263. Was a good Louis. Fought the Turks and was taken prisoner. His subjects thought 7,000,000 francs worth of him. Was awarded his halo for work in the Crusades. Not a patron of his ancestors. Very unpopular in Paris.

LOUIS X, 1289-1316. Reopened cafe's. Introduced the taxicab. Very popular.

LOUIS XI, 1423-1483. Fought England, and died too soon to hear of the discovery of the United States.

LOUIS XII, 1462-1515. Was king when the United States were discovered.

LOUIS XIII, 1601-1643. Permitted Cardinal Richelieu to king for him. Was a patron of cafe's, champagne, and Paris in general.

LOUIS XIV, called the Grand, 1638-1715. Furniture builder, salon decorator, wig maker, and constructor. Also assisted Paris in acquiring her reputation. Built Versailles, the Louvre, and Napoleon's tomb. He was the man who captured Alsace-Lorraine from Germany. (See Napoleon III.) Motto: I am the state. Ambition: Strauss waltzes at Versailles. Recreation: Dancing and attending to affairs of state. Address: Versailles.

LOUIS XV, 1710-1774, called a Bird. He lived during the reigns of Queens Pompadour and Du-Barry.

LOUIS XVI, 1754-1793. A Louis who continued the traditions of his ancestors, but--. Married Marie Antoinette. Introduced the turkey trot and the salome dance at Versailles. While his subjects were starving he ate pate de foies gras. They objected and carried his White Wigginess to Paris, where he ended his reign. Ambition: To have been any one of his ancestors, even No. 9. Recreation: Short walks in the jail yard. Address: Not permitted to receive letters. Epitaph: Easy Falls The Head Which Wore A Crown.

LOUIS XVII, 1785-1795. The only Louis who did not live long enough to have the good times of his ancestors, and the only Louis for whom the world has a word of sympathy.

LOUIS XVIII, 1775-1824, called the Last. He was the Louis who got back on the job after the dizziness of the Revolution and Napoleon had subsided.

LOVER, T. H. E., conqueror of worlds, architect of castles, lunatic, and saint. Spent early days only in living. In young manhood he met Her. From that moment all other hers he had known became lemons. L. was an expert prevaricator. Polished shoes, dressed neatly, shaved every day, and never ate onions. Spent evenings at Her house. Detested gas or electric lights. Was fond of the fireplace and hands. Quarreled occasionally. Spent salary for theatre tickets, candy, and flowers. Walked on air. Had a terrible time keeping away from his friends who wanted him to have a good time. One night Her looked wonderfully beautiful. L. said some things. He could not keep quiet. Her blushed, permitted him to sit closer, and then told L. he was the dearest, sweetest, finest, biggest, noblest, bravest lovey in the wide, wide world. Later L. secured an embarrassing interview and visited a jewelry store. Diet: Poor. Ambition: A mother-in-law. Address: Her home. Clubs: None. Epitaph: For Men May Come and Men May Go.

LUTHER, Martin, a German who started competition.

CHAPTER M

MCGINTY, a celebrated Irish diver.

McGRAW, John J., Manager of the New York Baseball organization, frequently used by the Philadelphia Athletics to gain the world's championship.

MACBETH, Lady, a royal somnambulist.

MACKINTOSH, discoverer of a method of keeping dry outside on a rainy day.

MAGELLAN, the man who got into straits and straights.

MAN, Sand, an old fellow who visits houses blessed with a child. Only calls after supper. Tells the little one he has played enough for the day, and sprinkles some sand in his eyes. When M. departs the little bundle is asleep in the nursery or all cuddled up in Mother's lap. Ambition: Sand for the older folks.

MANUEL, King, of England, and late of Portugal. Introduced Parisian life into Lisbon. Was a very sweet and very wise young man. Overlooked the fact that a king may rule a nation, but frequently is a poor press agent. Became incensed at his army and subjects. Moved in haste. Ambition: Lisbon and a dancing queen. Recreation: Watch bill-boards. Address: Watch bill-boards. Clubs: Down and Out. Epitaph: A Manuel And His Kingdom Are Soon Parted.

MARAT, one of the fathers of the French Revolution, who could rule a city, but not a woman.

MARCEL, Madame, of France. Discovered a good excuse for women to gaze in mirrors. Also caused heartfailure on a rainy day.

MARCONI, Guglielmo, the man who made the inventors of telegraph poles and wires look foolish. His inventions have made it possible for New York stock brokers to continue their business while journeying to Paris.

MARINER, A., traveler, albatross raiser. Gathered fame by making a voyage with some dead ones. His feat has frequently been duplicated on liners out of the regular tourist season.

MARK, Saint, of Venice. Guarded the pigeons of his square and the tourist who dwelt within his canals.

MARTINI, manufacturer of an American before-dinner drink which tastes too good.

MARY, a young girl who was presented with a famous lamb. Seldom was seen without the animal. Conveyed it to school with her one day, thus causing considerable mirth among the pupils. Was severely reprimanded by the teacher, as it was against the regulations of the institution to permit animals, other than the children, in the class-rooms. M. returned the lamb to the stable. Her biography has been extensively published.

MATERLINCK, a Belgian who believed the best way to get "copy" about himself into the newspapers was to try to keep it out. Recreation: Bluebird raising.

MAXIM, patron saint of the American-English tourist in Paris, who introduced New York prices into a naughty cafe. When a young man he discovered that the tourists were not paying enough money to see the sights. With the assistance of some handsomely gowned women he opened a cafe on the Rue Royal where they could. For years it was patronized by his countrymen until they were ruined. Later only royalty and tourists were permitted to enter and form a mistaken idea of the real French cafe, pay double prices for everything, see a few chorus girls, hear champagne bottles, and talk to English-speaking waiters. Ambition: Americans. Recreation: Staying at home. Press Agent: The Merry Widow and the Girl from Maxims. Epitaph: Honi Soit Qui Mal y Pense.

MAXIM, no relation of the above, as he only manufactured things to kill people, and not to financially ruin them.

MEDICI, Katie, an Italian French woman whose past was uncovered by those historians. Was fond of poison, but did not care for Methodists or Presbyterians.

MEDUSA, a celebrated ancient who had the delirium tremens in an acute stage.

MELLIN, he was the man who tried to cheat the baby out of the bottle.

MENDELSSOHN, wrote a tune which is usually played when a man goes to his fate.

MENNEN, the manufacturer of a baby and good complexion perquisite. Nothing like it for your face after shaving. His picture has been widely distributed, but never admired.

MERCURY, errand boy for the gods. Wore a pair of winged feet and feathers in his hat. Was also an artist's model. Ambition: A telegraph. Recreation: Same as the gods. Address: General delivery.

METHUSELAH, an ancient who was not like one in a thousand.

MICHEL, Saint, he kicked the devil out of paradise, and was instantly made the patron saint of France.

MIKE, Pat's partner (see Pat).

MILTON, John, wrote a Dante book, the title of which is known by everybody and the contents by few.

MOET and CHANDON, two competitors of Mr. Mumm who did much to bring the price of champagne to within the reach of millionaires.

MOHAMMED, inventor of the harem, and the man who introduced mormonism into Arabia. (See B. Young.) Also manufactured crescents, religion, and made Mecca the mecca for everything. Early life spent in business. This did not pay. He then married a widow and retired. Took up religion as a hobby. Became a professional. Found the sword was mightier than his kin. His salvation army was successful. His prisoners were given the alternative of a finely tempered, beauti-fully inlaid damascus blade or Islam. They always became fervently religious. Later M. embarked on a marrying campaign with equal success. Publications: The Koran, a treatise on everything. Ambition: The crescent on every flag. Recreation: Walking toward mountains; stroking his beard. Address: 23 Blvd. Allah, Mecca, Arabia. Epitaph: A Man's Works Take After Him.

MOLIERE, Jean B. P., a French author who wrote a few plays we do not have to see alone.

MONROE, James, the founder of a doctrine, the practicability of which nations desire to learn, and yet do not wish to make the test.

MORSE, Samuel G., an inventor who might have used his talents in other lines had Marconi lived before his time.

MOSES, whose whereabouts in the dark has puzzled all generations. Born in the bullrushes of Egypt. Entered politics as the son of Pharaoh's daughter and the leader of the Ghetto. When M. waxed astute, after the manner of his people, he discovered there were not sufficient shekels for himself and countrymen in the land of Egypt. He pleaded and plagued the king for permission to close the pawn shops and clothing stores. Now in those days the children of Egypt were wont to patronize the bazaars of the children of the Chosen, and Pharaoh was wroth within himself and refused the passports. The brave rabbi closed the kosher meat stores and took ship's leave. Adopting an original compass, he made forced marches to the Red Sea. Here the synagogue was overtaken by Pharaoh and his army. M. spilled the sea on them and marched on. From this time the journey to the Promised Land was slow. Whether this was due to good business or sore feet history does not relate. M. later climbed a mountain and received the ten commandments. After breaking them he returned to camp. He died before the journey was complete. Publications: Histories. Ambition: A railroad from Cairo to Jerusalem. Recreation: Tennis and camel racing. Also enjoyed tent life. Address: Care of Jewish Legation.

MOSES, Holy, no relation of the above. He was the fellow who came around when you hit your finger with the hammer.

MULLER, Maud, one of the few country girls who never went to New York City.

MUMM,[1] the man who made the most expensive drink on earth. The products of his cellars are frequently purchased by persons who cannot afford them. They form one of the principal ingredients of a good time (see Paris).

MUNCHAUSEN, Baron, traveler, explorer. While many of his books, lectures, and newspaper interviews have been questioned by scientific men, he is held in high regard due to his failure to claim the discovery of the north pole.

MUNYON, Doctor, an American herb doctor and optimist. Held the theory that while there was life there was a chance to sell some of his medicine.

MURPHY, Charles J. See What's Who of New York City.

---

[1] Ed. Note: The editor is personally responsible for the above stated facts.

CHAPTER N

NAPOLEON, a little Frenchman who wore a big hat, a little curl on his forehead, and whose ambitions were larger than his good luck. Started life by placing Corsica on the map. Like all great men, he was the dunce at school. Later he used his masters and prize-winning chums as first-row soldiers. Entered the army. Never succeeded as a sentry. Frequently amused himself by taking a couple of soldiers and capturing a city or an army between meals. The politicians in Paris saw the young man was not without talents. They gave him a few more soldiers. Then he went after countries. Captured Egypt, but had trouble with one Nelson of England. N. became unpopular with his neighbors. They all attacked him. He attacked them all. That settled it. He ate wars. After the powers were powerless N. scampered about Europe adding countries to France. He devoured Germany. Went after Russia, but they made it too hot and too cold for him. Had more trouble with that man Nelson. Became rich and divorced. Introduced Roosevelt publicity tactics into France and carried a third term. Started things. Began quarreling again. At last he was cooped up in Paris, and flew the white flag. Visited Elba. Revisited France. Started things again. Took some veterans to Belgium. There he was met by another Englishman by the name of Wellington who introduced him to Waterloo. For his kindness in leaving Europe England presented N. with a whole island, a complementary guard, and paid all his living expenses for six years. Later N. became responsible for one of the sights of Paris. Always carried his right hand in the front of his coat. Ambition: A French Nelson, England, and progeny. Recreation: Walking along the shore. Address: Fontainbleau, Europe, and At

Sea. Epitaph: I Desire That My Ashes Shall Rest On The Banks Of The Seine Among The Few French People I Did Not Take To War.

NAPOLEON II. Absent.

NAPOLEON III. He was the man who did not devour Germany. Ambition: Rough on rats for the Kaiser and Bismarck. Recreation: Travel. Address: Paris when the Dutchmen would permit him. Epitaph: Here Lies A Napoleon, But No Bonaparte.

NARCISSUS, a lover who forgot there were other girls, and pined away into a flower and a tiresome song.

NATION, Carrie, a window-smashing American liquor suffragette who believed the ridiculous doctrine that all men should be sober all the time.

NEBUCHADNEZZAR, King, an old king whose name is blamed hard to spell.

NEPTUNE, boss of the seas. Has charge of the Atlantic liners, wireless, and the seasick. Ambition: A bridge from London to New York. Recreation: Storms. Address: Atlantic. Clubs: Yacht.

NERO (first name forgotten). A Roman emperor who thought nothing burned like a good tarred Christian. Also made fire departments a necessity in the Eternal City. Ambition: A good show in the Colosseum. Recreation: Fiddling. Clubs: Chorus Girls. Epitaph: For He Was A Jolly Good Fellow.

NERO, Mrs., Nero's wife, who had considerable trouble with her husband.

NEWTON, Isaac, a man who was knighted for propounding the theory that it is easier to wait under a tree for an apple to fall than to climb after it.

NIC, Old, a friend of everybody, no matter who turns them down. Will stick to you clear to the end. One of those good souls who never fails to give encouragement and grasp you by the hand when you want to do something you know you should not do. Was driven from home when a young man. Set up competition and succeeded wonderfully. Organized the largest community in existence. This is steadily growing despite considerable opposition. N. numbers among his friends most of the great people who ever lived. He is counting on others. Caused much worry to mothers and wives, but seldom troubled the men. Publications: French literature; some fine books and pictures. Occupation: Looking for idle hands. Ambition: You. Recreation: Theatres, cabarets, music halls, cafe's, champagne, Mone Carlo, etc. Fond of chorus girls. Address: Paris. N. also travels extensively. Epitaph: Ad Infinitum.

NIMROD, the first grouse, pheasant, and deer hunter who succeeded without the advantages of a gun, a game preserve, or a license.

NOAH, ship-builder, animal tamer. A fine old ancestor who had considerable to do in preserving the race for we posterity. When a young man he shunned the ways of young men, and never sat in the seat of the scornful. Studied shipbuilding on the Clyde and designed the largest floating stable on record. Made quite a reputation as an animal collector. Took to the sea when well advanced in years. N. was the first man to descend Mt. Ararat without first making the ascension. Publications: The Log of the Ark. Ambition: No more floods, or a larger crew. Recreation: Bridge. Address: Care of the Editor. Clubs: Yacht. Epitaph: De Profundis.

NOBLE, A., of Norway, the inventor of the black hand and labor union weapon. His invention also made possible the premature discharge of dynamite and the awarding of the Noble prizes.

CHAPTER O

O'CONNELL, Dan, said to have been an Irishman. Probably born in Dublin, raised in Dublin. Raised cain in Dublin. Repealed in Dublin. Dublined in Dublin. Died in Dublin. Tradition connects his name with the early stages of the home rule bill. Ambition: Ireland south of Ulster. Recreation: Oratory. Address: Dublin. Clubs: Dublin. Favorite Color: Green.

O'GRADY, Sweet Rosie, also of Ireland, long dead, but still bragged about.

ORANGE, William of, also of Ireland. He was the man who made it a crime to wear the color named after him on the seventeenth of March. (See St. Patrick.)

ORPHEUS, lutist. When a young man he was given a lute. Practised in obscurity, and later appeared before large audiences. Made several successful concert tours. Married Eurydice. Spent a happy honeymoon. The bride did not wear shoes. She was bitten by a serpent. She died. O. descended to the abode of Old Nic, and charmed him with some Grecian ragtime. Nic promised to return the lady if O. would promise to get out of the place without looking around to see what other respectable people were there. O. started for the door. He heard familiar voices and rubbered. That ended the contract, and for all the editor has been able to ascertain Eurydice is there to this day.

OSTLER, William, a doctor who was knighted for proposing that all fossils should be ostlerized. Ambition: To murder the men who got that story into print. Recreation: Medicine. Address: Oxford. Epitaph: He Practised, But Not What He Preached.

OTHELLO, of Venice. Born in Morocco. Went to Venice and fell in love with one Desdemona, an Italian girl. They were married. Mrs. Othello lost one of her favorite handkerchiefs and was killed by her enraged husband. Shakespeare, of England, a writer, heard of the incident and made some money out of it.

CHAPTER P

PADEREWSKI, Ignace Jan, another farewell-concert giver, who wore long red hair, a soulful expression, insured his fingers, and broke pianos.

PALLAS, a Grecian goddess who was metamorphosed into a raven perch by Poe.

PAN, monstrosity, musical instrument maker, friend of poets. Born half a man and half a goat. Took after the latter. Studied music under the old masters and outfluted Apollo. Was also a sheep fancier. Fathered fife and drum corps. Ambition: A pair of shoes or a goat's appetite. Recreation: Hunting and falling in love. Address: Greece. Clubs: Musical.

PAN, Peter, a little fellow who was a delightful actress, believed in fairies, and crowded houses in England and the United States.

PANKHURST, Mrs., a celebrated English woman who terrorized a government, starved herself, smashed windows, blew up things, and made speeches for a living. Girlhood spent in developing muscle, pluck, and theories. She appeared before the public and declared that the liquor traffic would be terminated when women voted. Spent years of her life wondering why the men would not give them the privilege. Never cared for the ministry, although she was a very good woman. Ambition: A woman king. "Votes for Women" in the Union Jack. Recreation: Planning the "next." Publications: From the Cradle to the Ballot. Windows I have Smashed. Address: London. Care Scotland Yard.

PANKHURST, Sylvia, a little Pankhurst who helps mamma break things.

PANZA, Sancho, Don Quixote's interlocutor and stable boss.

PARIS, son of the King of Tyre, who ran away with another man's wife named Helen. A city in France has been named to do him honor.

PARNELL, C. S., father of the downfall of English ministries and Ulster. Born of Irish parents. First man to successfully explode dynamite in Parliament without being executed. Ambition: An Ulsterless Ireland, a Conservativeless England. Address: Close to the English ministry. Epitaph: The Bills Men Introduced Live After Them.

PARSIFAL, the longest-winded singer who ever stepped on an opera stage.

PASTEUR, Doctor, discoverer. Experimented with mad dogs until he came to the conclusion they should be shot or chained. A subway station in Paris has been named after him.

PATRICK, Saint, a Scotchman who drove all the snakes out of Ireland with the exception of those in bottles. Also introduced the brogue and the shamrock into the Emerald Isle.

PAT, also of Ireland. At an early age he emigrated to the United States. There he took up the hod-carrying business. Went on the stage and set the world laughing. He also entered politics, captured the American police force, and, together with his brothers in Parliament, rules Great Britain and the United States.

PATTI, Adelina, a singer who said au revoir but not good bye. Epitaph: Cum Grano Salis.

PEAR,[1] the man who names most of the London busses, and keeps the people of England clean for a penny a week. His business is international with the exception of Glasgow and Italy.

PEARY, Captain Robert E., explorer who said he reached the north pole and convinced a few people. Was also forced to write a book and lecture. Publications: How Dr. Cook Almost Got Ahead of Me. Ambition: That a certain man had not made him get all the way there the last time. Grave: The Cook incident.

PENN, William, a man whose picture appears on all Quaker Oats boxes. An Englishman who left his country, bought Pennsylvania, built the slow, old town of Philadelphia, and hung up the American Liberty Bell.

PERICLES, of Athens. Political boss, philosopher, and general. Secured his reputation through brains, a voice, and a well-oiled political machine. Started the golden age of Greece with a loud blast of the horn of plenty.

PETER, no relation to the following. He introduced the art of chocolate making into Switzerland, and the art of eating it into America. Ambition: More children and people with sweet teeth.

PETER, Saint, a fine old bearded saint who is an excellent bookkeeper, and a detester of roosters. A church in Rome has taken his name. Ambition: A new key. Recreation: Oiling hinges. Address: Golden gates.

---

[1] Ed. Note: This is not an advertisement. The editor does not use soap.

PHARAOH, of Egypt. Benefactor of Moses and Joseph. Was also the father of Pharaoh's daughter. Built a few pyramids, cigarette factories, and made a handsome mummy.

PHILIP II, a king of Spain who, with an armada to press his suit, endeavored to marry a queen of England. Both the suit and the armada were left in the bay of Biscay, and the queen an old maid. Ambition: To the Inquisition with all Englishmen. Motto: Faint heart never won fair lady. Address: Spain.

PINAUD, Edward, discoverer of the only thing which would have saved your hair.

PINKHAM, Lydia, of vegetable compound fame. Made a fortune out of advertisements, little boxes of pills, and women who believed what they read.

PIPER, Peter, famous picker of pickled peppers. Also held accounts against many people. Caused considerable worry to his creditors.

PITMAN, Isaac, discovered a method of making political speakers more careful of what they said. His invention has secured wealthy husbands for many a pretty and poor stenographer.

PLUTARCH, the only man who had more lives than a cat.

PLUTO, boss of the underworld until Old Nic got on the job. Also the manufacturer of a morning beverage.

PLUVIUS, E., was the fellow who always made it rain when you wanted to wear your new hat or go to a ball game.

POE, Ed. A., an American poet who specialized in ravens and cold chills.

POINCAIRE, Raymond, a Frenchman who has a splendid opportunity to get out of this book.

POLLUX, Leda's other twin. (See Mother and Brother.)

POLO, Marco, F. R. G. S., traveler, discoverer, and lecturer. Began expeditions from Venice. Discovered China, Japan, and the Orient. Returned to Venice and Doctor Cooked his neighbors. He is supposed, however, to have visited the countries, as he produced a pair of chop sticks, a Chinese laundry, and some Japanese lanterns. These were accepted as proofs by the University of Venice. Ambition: The north pole.

POMPADOUR, Madame, coiffeur, Queen of France. Said to have been a peach. Was a great friend of Louis XV, and helped make the dances at Versailles a success. Ambition: Plenty of hair. Recreation: Versailles. Address: See Louis. Clubs: Anti.

POWELL-BADEN, Robert S., a warrior who retired from service and invented soldiers to be shot when the next big war comes along.

PROCRASTINATOR, T. H. E., an extinct man who believed in the doctrine of To-morrow. He was a thief, but was never convicted. Ancient records state he invariably had an excuse for present inactivity, but would promise results the following day. Was a close friend of Failure. Put off everything except Death, and even did his best to keep him away as long as possible. Motto: No time like the future. Ambition: To accomplish to-morrow what the other fellow is doing to-day. Recreation: Always before business. Address: Nobody knows. Clubs: Many.

PROGRESS, Pilgrim, an Englishman who made an extensive journey encumbered with a large pack. He visited Paris, had some hairbreadth escapes, was stuck in the mud, but finally returned and became respectable like all other Englishmen.

PUCCINI, Giacomo, maker of tunes and curtain calls. A musician who did not starve, and who gave the classical name "La Faniculla del West" to the plain "girl of the golden west."

PULLMAN, an American who invented an expensive means of travel. P. also is responsible for the vast fortunes acquired by porters.

PUNCH, husband of Judy, and a great favorite with the children, even if he did beat his old wife. Led a hen-pecked life. Traveled in several European countries and spoke all the best-selling languages. His name has been given to a serious London publication.

PYTHAGORAS, a Greek who said some people would be pigs after they were dead.

CHAPTER Q[1]

QUIETUS, Fluvius, of Rome. Always put his name to everything when he came around.

QUIXOTE, Don, famous knight-errant of Spain. Made some desperate conquests for his lady-love, and was defeated by a windmill. In all his defeats, however, he showed to the world that a laugh cuts deeper than a sword, and that satire would kill where a lance could not penetrate. The word quixotic is used to his commemoration.

---

[1] Ed. Note: The editor apologizes for the few Q's who have been famous.

CHAPTER R[1]

RALEIGH, Walt., one of the men who was permitted to hold hands with Queen Elizabeth. His other feats were the introduction of the pipe into England and the plug into Ireland.

RAMESES II, an Egyptian king who went about building burial mountains, statues to himself, and permitting cigarettes to be named after him.

RAPHAEL, a decorator who took paint in its raw state and made it worth money. Filled walls, principally in Italy, with some expensive paintings, and, like Angelo, used the Vatican as his studio. Ambition: Churches with larger walls. Recreation: Painting, art, and canvas weaving. Address: All galleries.

RECAMIER, Madame, of Paris. Supplied the society column to the newspapers. To be invited to her salon meant that you would get plenty to eat, that you were somebody, that you would see somebody, and that you would have to wear your Sunday clothes. Her R. S. V. P.'s were always accepted. R. finally lost her money, and with it her friends. Ambition: The man of the hour. Epitaph: When She Had It She Spent It.

REMBRANDT, Dutch painter who specialized in portraits of old ladies and Rembrandt. Also brought considerable fame down upon himself by filling a museum in Amsterdam with tourist-drawing paintings.

---

[1] Ed. Note: The editor apologizes for the character of the R's who have been famous.

REMINGTON, the man who invented a typewriter at which many pretty stenographers[1] sit.

REVIEWER, The Book, he is the fellow who said a chef-d'oeuvre like Who Was Who should be used for ballast.

RHODES, Cecil, a poor boy who saved his money and purchased South Africa.

RHODES, Colossus of, a giant of antiquity who was not killed by a stone. He rusted to death.

RICHELIEU, Cardinal, the man who held down the throne for Louis XIII, and disagreed with the Duke of Buckingham.

RITZ, innkeeper who made hotels in which we all would like to stop, but cannot. Ambition: Americans and English nobility. Recreation: Visiting his hotels. Address: Ritz and Carlton. Clubs: Does not need any.

ROBESPIERRE, a French politician who had the opportunity of doing to his enemies what most politicians would like to do to theirs. Was finally voted out and down.

ROBINSON, Jack, brother of Sam Hill. He claimed distinction simply because some people were sufficiently clever to do things before his name could be pronounced.

ROCKEFELLER, John D., an American who endeavored to drive his camel through the eye of a needle by giving advice, building churches and colleges, and squeezing competitors. Like all millionaires, he was born penniless. R. worked hard, helped the

---

[1] Ed. Note: Advertisement for the stenographers, not the machine.

missions out of his $3 a week, married, and purchased some oil fields. He struck oil. He made it in a trust. Then he began purchasing colleges to keep young men out of business. As his wealth increased his stomach and hair wore out. Could make seven people dizzy thinking of his money. Spent the latter portion of his life dodging subpoenae servers, and doubling his fortune by the dissolution of his business. Ambition: More churches, colleges, and less competition. Also another Supreme Court decision. Recreation: Golf, the coiffeurs, and telling young men of the futility of competition. Address: Courts and church. Clubs: Y. M. C. A., when he can spare the time from his legal and congressional investigations.

ROCKEFELLER, John D., Jr., the little Rockefeller who will have the fun of spending it. He was a good boy, and told other young men how fortunate they were in being born poor and all about the fungus which grows on the root of all evil. Never knew what a good time he could have with his Dad's coin in Paris. Ambition: To be like father. Recreation: Sunday school. Occupation: Forming new trusts and enlarging the old ones. Clubs: Y. M. C.A.

RODIN, August, a Frenchman who did his utmost to fill European and American galleries with statues at a price which would have made Mike Angelo a billionaire.

ROJESVENSKY, Admiral, a great Russian admiral and sea fighter who gloriously defeated the fishing squadron in the English Channel. Later hit a snag in the Orient.

ROMEO, Juliet's best fellow, who learned that his road to true love ended in a cemetery.

ROMULUS, Remus' twin. Collaborated with his brother in home life and in building Rome.

ROOSEVELT, Theodore, nom de plume, T. R., Teddy, press agent, The Outlook, "I," traveler, teddy bear manufacturer, lecturer, interview giver, museum collector, "ME," Guildhall orator, dee-lighted, "MYSELF," mooser, hunter, band-wagon driver, band-wagon, Panama canal, rough rider, circus leader, circus, down-with-rafter, and a former retired and retiring president of the United States. When a young man he spent his father's money by going to college, shooting lions, and raising a large family. During the Spanish-American War he employed a troop of rough riders, stormed San Juan Hill, and got into the newspapers. Made up his mind he would stay there. R. became governor of New York State with ambitions. Being a wealthy man, and capable of contributing to the cause of the Republican party, he was elected vice-president of the United States. A hand other than his own made him president. Here his newspaper career really began. R. first opened a three-ring circus in the White House, wore a rough rider hat, and told the country what a great president he was. The voters believed him, and did not object to four years more. During this administration R. successfully advertised himself, the family, started the Panama Canal, and appointed one William Howard Taft (see Poor Bill) his successor. R. then traveled through Africa with a magnificent body guard of photographers and newspaper men. After shooting a museum-full of specimens, he toured Europe and told the king how to king and the emperors how to emp. Returning to the United States he placed his hand in state politics. Fingers were badly burned. When it came time to elect another president, R. was tired of scene shifting and yearned for the bouquets of the audience. He girded up his loins with the robes of sanctity, placed an international Harvester Trust halo over his head, and proclaimed himself a second Moses who was destined to lead the children of America out of the Land of the Frying Pan into that of the Fire. With a mighty army of politicians, who also wanted to get back, R. started his campaign with such a huge band he could not hear any others. The fight was based on telling the voters how easily they had been deceived four years earlier in what he had told them concerning that "molycoddle Taft." R. was elected by the greatest majority in history until the ballots were hatched. Later he joined the ranks of William Jennings Bryan. Publications: The "I" books. Ambition: To get back into Who's Who and Washington. Address: The Outlook. Oyster Bay for newspapermen. Clubs: Founder of the Ananias. Epitaph: Same as Bryan's.

ROTHSCHILDS, the Morgan-Rockefellers of Europe without quite as much money.

ROY, Robert, a very wicked Scotchman whom we all hope will always escape the police.

RUBENS, P. P., an artist who realized styles frequently changed, and therefore painted fat people without their clothes.

RUSSE, Charlotte, a pleasant creature, but one who sometimes caused pain after a visit.

RUSSIA, T. H. E., Czar of, an anti-bomb loving monarch with modern subjects and a tenth-century brain. His childhood was spent in a steel-lined cage, guarded by the army and the fleet. He was crowned in a bomb-proof church by a thoroughly searched clergyman, only the crown, the crowner, and the crowned being present to witness the ceremony. Seldom goes about the country, as he fears the heartfelt expressions of his subjects. In 1908 he became mixed up with Japan. Is now economizing. Ambition: Only life. Recreation: Dissolving Doumas. signing death warrants. Address: Large packages are always opened by the servants. Send letters care St. Petersburg police department. Clubs: Army. Epitaph: It Is A Wonder He Did Not Have This Long Ago.

CHAPTER S

SALOME, a celebrated dancer who could fill the largest opera houses in the world with bald heads, opera glasses, and jealous women. She is still in Who's Who, and probably will remain there until arrested.

SAM, Uncle, a tall, lean, good-natured rich man who sets paces and spends his money. Born July 4, 1776, S. Great Britain. Godfathered by France. Was an impetuous baby. Education: School of experience at Washington. S. was assisted in early life by a number of men who took an interest in him. When thirty-six years of age he chastised his mother, but later became on excellent terms. Went in for land and colonization business. Succeeded. At the age of eighty-four S. suffered from a severe attack of internal indiscretion. Recuperated slowly. Later entered the trust-raising business, and devoted considerable time to politics. In 1897 he spanked a European power, but had to take care of the children after the incident. S. is either Republican or Democratic. Favors the former, although once in awhile he desires change. Wore a goatee, long hair, high hat, a suit made out of the flag, smoked cigarettes, had bad manners, and used much slang. Publications: Bank notes. Ambition: Another Republican president. Address: Washington, D. C., U. S. A. Epitaph: (If he ever gets one he deserves it.)

SAMSON, exponent of hair restorer and an iconoclast. When a young man he rehearsed his muscles until he could break a chain and lift a fat lady. Entered the army. Was successful until he became bald. Committed suicide by pushing a temple on himself.

SANDOW, a pupil of the above, vaudeville star and coin collector. One of those individuals whom nature has endowed with a magnificent body, and sufficient brains to make money with it.

SANTOS-DUMONT, a pre-Zeppelin-Wright air investigator who had enough money and sense to quit before people remarked how natural he looked.

SAVONAROLA, a reformer of Florence, Italy, who succeeded in closing the cafe's, theatres, and dance halls. He was popular with the masses until election day. When the opposition returned they made it hot for him.

SAWYER, Thomas, a plain American boy who was rescued from obscurity by Mark Twain, and became a good salesman.

SCHLITZ, press agent of Milwaukee, U. S. A., who was successful in advertising himself and his town. In England he is Schwepps.

SCHOPENHAUER, father of race suicide. Lionized by the French Republic and T. R. Ambition: Empty cribs. Recreation: Trips with his wife and children. Clubs: Mother's.

SCOTS, Mary Queen of, a Scotch lady who is said to have been beautiful, who fell in love, and was one of the few women whose less attractive sister got the better of her.

SCOTT, Walter, a Scotchman who secured fame without adopting the national characteristics. His critics claim this was the reason he failed in business. Wrote some books which are read by students and persons possessing much time.

SEBASTIAN, Saint, the Italian who was shot with arrows and ran second to the apostles in the number of his portraits exhibited in European galleries.

SEIDLITZ, powder manufacturer.

SEVILLE, Barber of, a celebrated tonsorial artist who introduced the marcel wave and the Gillette razor into Spain.

SHACKLETON, Ernest, another pole explorer. He was saved the ignominy of reaching the desired point by the shortness of rations, but he was near enough to become a profitable author and lecturer.

SHAKESPEARE, William, the man who was born at Stratford-on-Avon. When a young man he amused himself by poaching, visiting the Hathaway cottage, and being the village pest. Married the inmate of the cottage and went to London, a city in England. S. became an apprentice actor, and was said to have been nearly as bad an actor as his contemporaries. His fame later arose due to his growing popularity. He died. S.'s birthplace is now one of the tourist sights of the world. More postcards are sent from this town than from any of its size in Europe. The church where he lies buried has an immense floating congregation. S. also shared honors with one Bacon for writing a few plays. Ambition: Present-day prices in Elizabethan theatres. Recreation: Rehearsals. Address: The World. Epitaph: (Has been obliterated.)

SHAMPOO, a barber of Shoo Poo, China, who introduced the art of clean heads into the Celestial Empire. This has since fallen into disrepute in that country, but is sometimes practiced in other lands.

SHAW, G. Bernard, grouch, truth teller. An English writer who made money by being honest enough to tell people what they knew. S.'s enemies claim he would have to work should his theories be put into practice. Believes in socialism and wants everything. Author of considerable sarcasm, wit, and divided opinion as to his talents. Ambition: An Americanless England. Also, sales. Address: Watch bill-boards.

SHEBA, Queen of, an ancient mere woman who matched her brains against the brainiest man who ever lived. She lost.

SHEM, Noah's heir. Was first officer of the Ark.

SHERMAN, General, secured his fame by marching to the sea and giving a terse definition of war.

SHERRY, proprietor of a New York restaurant where a person feels wealthy while at the table and poor afterward.

SHOE, Old Woman of the, one of those anti-race-suicide mothers whose family caused considerable worry. Ambition: A better job for her husband. Address: Shoe. Clubs: She did not have time for any, and thus could not be a suffragette.

SHUSTER, Morgan, an American child who attempted to play the diplomatic game in Persia with grown ups. Was spanked and sent home. Occupation: Crying. Ambition: Ambassador to a country without diplomats. Address: Home.

SHYLOCK. See New York City business directory.

SIMON, Simple, epicurean. Passed an uneventful life with the exception of an encounter with a confectioner near the fair grounds. The man operated his business on a cash basis. Simon was broke and no sale was consummated.

SINBAD, an old tar whose yarns are still on the distaff.

SISTERS, Seven Sutherland, a noted family who held out salvation for the bald and envy to women.

SMITH, John, the bravest man who ever lived. Smith ate the first lobster.

SMITH, John, secured his renown for living in every city in the world.

SOCRATES. He helped introduce brains into Greece. Committed suicide.

SOLOMON, King, author, musician, builder, benedict. An old Mormon who established a record for wearing wedding clothes. When a child he developed a Boston brain. This grew as the years advanced. At a tender age he began acquiring mothers-in-law. This caused his subjects to doubt his acumen. S. thoroughly vindicated himself, and set about building a city and a big church to hold his family. Wrote a number of popular songs. His proverbs also had a big sale. Ambition: Just one more wife and an end to those quarrels in the harem. Recreations: Picnics with the family. Also was fond of the phonograph. Address: Care the Mrss. Solomon. Epitaph: Here Lies The Original Man Who Knew It All.

SON, Prodigal, tourist, oat sower, and herdsman. Son of wealthy parents. Became tired of home and desired to travel. Visited foreign lands and had a jolly good time. His letter of credit expired. Friends were never at home after the event. S. had to work. Later he took a bath and walked home. Father was delighted and gave a banquet in his honor. Unpopular with his brother. Career: Wild. Satisfaction: Saw something of life. Address: Home.

SOUSA, John P., American bandmaster who wrote books and shot pigeons between march compositions.

SPENCER, Herbert, a scientist who believed the human race degenerated from monkeys, and established the theory that only the survivors are the fittest.

SUFFRAGETTE, T. H. E., a woman who lived years ago in Great Britain and the United States, who believed that noble man was incompetent, incomplete, incompatible, incongruent, inconsistent, and an incubus in his incurious incumbency. She was the daughter of Too Much Time and Too Much Money. Early days spent at home. She married and began her career. S.'s first weakness was a club. Then she fell to the level of a speech maker and a flag carrier. The fanatical desire to see her name in print led to the adoption of strenuous press-agent tactics. She died fighting. Ambition: To offset her husband's vote on election day. Recreation: Parading, windows, bombs, letter boxes, English ministries, and a string of etcs. Epitaph: Requiescat In Pace. (Also see Mrs. Pankhurst and Hope.)

SUFFRAGETTE, T. H. E. Anti-, still lives, but is dying fast. Belongs to the moss-back half of femininity. Has serious objection to use of her head, except for decorative purposes. Was not averse to press notices and looked with envy on the achievements of the suffragettes in this direction. Being denied high office in their ranks because of lack of adequate cerebration, she set up a rival organization where brains were not requisite. Entertains the utterly absurd idea that all women, except herself, belong at home with their husbands and children. Where they belong in the absence of these, deponent sayeth not. Ambition: Continued parasitic existence. Recreation: Manufacturing evidence and tagging on behind. Address: Wherever there are suffrage meetings. Epitaph: Alas! The World Does Move And She Was "Agin It."

SULZER, William, the kettle who called Murphy black. Also the governor of New York who enjoyed the unprecedented honor of retiring from office in order that he might be considered a progressive. Motto: Be sure your sins will get you out. Ambition: To be a martyr to the claws. Diet: Tigers. Epitaph: You May Air, You May Perfume Your Clothes As You Will, But The Smell Of Impeachment Will Cling To You Still.

CHAPTER T

TAFT, William Howard, a former fat, and last Republican, president of the United States who worshipped the trusts, the Constitution, the Supreme Court, and Theodore Roosevelt. The love he bore the latter resulted in his election. The two brothers quarreled because Bill would not step aside and let Teddy run things all over again. The two brothers fought and another ran away with the election. Principal events during T.'s administration: Roosevelt's trip, The Outlook, Oyster Bay, Standard Oil, That election. Ambition: 1916. Recreation: Golf, messages to Congress. Address: Cincinnati, O. Epitaph: How Sharper Than A Serpent's Tooth It Is To Have A Thankless Predecessor.

TANGLEFOOT, he was the man who first stuck flies on flypaper.

TANGUWAY, Eva, an actress who did not care even if those on the front row did.

TENNYSON, Lord, an English poet who turned a perpetual light on a charging brigade.

TERRY, Ellen, a dear old lady whom the world wishes the footlights might always shine upon and upon whom the curtain would never descend.

THAW, Harry K., famous lawyer endower. Entered life as the rich son of a wealthy father. Became interested in the stage at an early age, but only got as far as the chorus. Later performed on a New York roof garden. Alienists say he was the sanest crazy man and the craziest sane man who ever lived. Also obtained some publicity by expensive exploring in Canada and New Hampshire. Ambition: Wreaths for Jerome. Recreation: Straightening jackets. Address: See this morning's paper.

THEMISTOCLES, a Greek warrior who fought, but did not run a marathon.

THIRD, Richard the, a king of England who showed how much he thought of the country by offering to exchange it for any kind of a horse.

THUMB, Thomas, a white pygmy who enriched himself through his misfortunes and the curiosity of the world.

TIBERIUS, just a Roman emperor who fitted the job.

TIFFANY,[1] of New York City, London, and Paris. Introduced high prices into the jewelry business. Greatly admired by fiance's and millionaires. Has gained considerable fame, as his products will pawn on a good margin. Ambition: A man in love.

TIME, Father, a very old man who has been introduced to everybody. Very unpopular with the ladies. A great wound and sorrow healer, but unkind to the old. He went about the world changing babies into men and women, and placing gray hair and wrinkles where they were never wanted. Author: Of tears. Recreation: Reaping. Address: Your home. Epitaph: Ad Finem.

TINTORETTO, a Venetian painting manufacturer. Together with P. P. Rubens he held the record for covering canvas and wearing out brushes. Recreation: He never had any.

---

[1] Ed. Note: This is not an advertisement, as the editor is not an actress.

TITIAN, another painter of Venice. His works have always been popular with the men. They are exhibited in all European galleries, and cause consternation among clergymen and school teachers. T. certainly could paint. Ambition: Models. Recreation: Models.

TOLSTOY, a voice out of the dark.

TOM. (See Richard and Harry.)

TOM, Uncle, an old negro actor who appeared in every city, town, village, and hamlet in the United States north of the Confederate States. His history was written by Mrs. H. B. Stowe, and was the match which kindled the Civil War. The Northerners have since learned that all negroes are not Uncle Toms, and are wondering whether any mistakes were made back in 1861.

TOURISTS, T. H. E., a man and woman who carried a camera, bought post-cards, read Baedekers, visited Cook's office, rode in carriages, and then told their friends all about the trip. Ambition: Just one look at everything. Address: Principally Europe. Epitaph: They Came, They Saw, They Vanished.

TROY, Helen of, a peach of a girl who eloped with a man and caused the longest siege in history to make her elope back again.

TURNER, J. M. W., an English painter whose paint exploded on canvas.

TWAIN, Mark, an American who wore long white hair, made after-dinner speeches, received university degrees, and made people laugh.

TWINS, Siamese, two men who were closer than brothers.

TWIST, Oliver, one of those unfortunates whose history had to be divulged for the financial gain of a great writer and many theatrical mangers.

CHAPTER U

UFFIZI, an Italian who prevented scores of the old masters from starving to death by filling his house in Florence with their canvases. Since the Morgan art raid the market price has advanced and U.'s investment has become profitable.

ULYSSES, warrior, inventor, and traveler. Sprang into fame at the siege of Troy, where he invented the horse which recaptured Helen. Escaped from Polyphemus, a one-eyed giant, by sticking a burning telegraph pole in his eye. Later performed his greatest feat by evading the Sirens. Stayed away from home so much his wife forgot what he looked like. His dog, however, recalled the scent and prevented U. from sleeping in the barn. Press Agent: Homer. Recreation: Travel, wars. Address: Ithaca.

UNDERWOOD, Oscar, known as Underwood Bill. A gentleman from Alabama who walked in a presidential, but ran in a senatorial, race. He had something to do with the high cost of tariffing.

UNKNOWN, the man who painted thousands of pictures in art galleries.

CHAPTER V

VALESQUEZ, Spanish canvas coverer. In the absence of the camera, he was appointed the court oil photographer. Exposed a portrait of Philip IV in every gallery in the world. Art textbooks think a great deal of V.

VANDERBILT, an American family of means who possess a few railroads, much of New York City, some splendid divorces, and a weakness for Newport and newspapers.

VAN DYKE, beard inventor and artist. A Dutchman who invaded England with portraits and his tonsorial achievement.

VAN HOUTEN. He was the man who put cocoa in tin boxes.

VENUS, a dream of a girl who lived long ago, posed for her statue, and had to die after everybody fell in love with her. Was born and painted at sea. Married at an early age. Was a regular heart breaker. V. had an affair with one Adonis, and later with Vulcan. Not much is known of her old-ladyhood, as she refused to pose for statues when advanced in years. Ambition: Parisian gowns, the love of the gods. Recreation: Love. Address: The Louvre, Paris. The Uffizi Gallery, Florence. Clubs: She was too good looking to be a suffragette.

VERSONNESE, Paul, decorator of the Doges Palace, Venice, and contributor to most galleries. His work was nearly as prolific as Reubens, and two or three of his paintings compare favorably with the naughty Titian.

VESPASIAN, the man who built the colosseum in Rome for the tourists.

VESPUCCI, A., an enterprising journalist who arrived on the scene after the discovery had been made. V. wrote the story in such a clever manner he succeeded in cheating the discoverer out of naming the place. (See Columbus.)

VICTOR, he was the man who put the fox terrier in front of the talking machine.

VINCI, Leonardo Da, painted Mona Lisa for the Louvre, Paris. His reputation has soared in proportion to the duration of her absence. Ambition: To be the Morgan family painter. Recreation: Looking for purchasers. Epitaph: He Has Finished His Last Supper.

VIRGIL, an old text-book writer. Had something to do with the AEneid.

VIRGIN, Vestal, an old maid of Rome who was locked up in the forum for protection. She attended the gladiatorial contests and played with her thumbs.

VITUS, Saint, dancing master whose repertoire did not include the turkey trot.

VOLTAIRE, a Frenchman who went around with a bad taste in his mouth.

VULCAN, fireman and tinsmith. Made a number of celebrated forgings. Had a career like the ancients and fell in love with Venus.

CHAPTER W

WAGNER, Dick, a Dutchman who wrote a few sheets of music, went into the opera business, but died before the good singers or Hammerstein prices appeared.

WALKER, Johnnie, 1820. Spent most of his life at your favorite bar until you appeared.

WALTON, Isaac, he was the fellow who started those awful fish stories.

WASHINGTON, George, child model, father, etc. Spent early days chopping trees, holding conversations with his father, killing Indians, and being brave. Later he drove those tea-selling Englishmen from the United States, said farewell to his troops, and became a politician. W. decided he was not good enough for a third term and retired. His picture has been widely distributed. Ambition: To be the happy father of a big Uncle Sam. Recreation: Powdering his wig. Address: Washington. Clubs: Anti-Ananias.

WASHINGTON, Booker T., only a distant relation of the above. A big black man who went about the country raising money to put brains into ivory. He also told his audience how unfortunate they were in not being coons. (See Uncle Tom.)

WATSON, Doctor. He boswelled Sherlock Holmes.

WEBSTER, Dan., an American statesman and a member of Congress before the invention of investigating committees. He died famous.

WEBSTER, Noah, speller, writer, reference-book maker, and language itemizer. W. was the man to whom Mark Twain paid a glowing tribute by saying he was a great writer, but his stories were too short.

WELLINGTON, Duke of, an Englishman who taught a great French general to say "Tout est perdu." He later taught England that many a good soldier makes a poor politician.

WHITEHEAD, of Fiume, Austria. Mission in life was to reduce the size of dreadnaughts.

WHITTINGTON, Richard, proprietor of a celebrated back-fence walker.

WIDOW, Merry, a dream who hung around Mr. Maxim's restaurant in Paris, made love to nobility, toured the world, and finally died. Death was caused by overexertion. Before the war she was engaged to a Balkan prince. W. visited New York, London, and Paris. Everybody fell in love with her and whistled her praises. Past: (?) Press Agent: Frank Lehar. Ambition: Millionaires. Recreation: After 11.45 P. M. Epitaph: When Will There Be Another Like Her?

WIGGS, Mrs., a woman who successfully advertised cabbages.

WILLIAMS. He was the man who ruined the shaving-mug business.

WILSON, Puddin' Head, a young lawyer who was fathered by Mark Twain. No relation to the following.

WILSON, Woodrow, one time president of an American football, educational institution, who outgrew his job. He moved up to be governor, made a few cure-all speeches, introduced Roosevelt to Bryan, changed his address to Washington. Took out a watchful, waiting policy. Is now in Who's Who, but whether he will remain in that publication or this one cannot be determined at the time of going to press. Ambition: To keep Roosevelt and Bryan running. Recreation: Teaching, Browning, other brain exercises, thinking, Congress. Address: Washington, care Joseph Tumulty. Clubs: Pedagogue, Mexican.

WINSLOW, Mrs., known over the world as the lady who soothes the baby's little tummie.

WONDERLAND, Alice of, traveless discoveress. Made a lady of the Royal Geographical Society. She was a great favorite of the children and many grown ups. She always will remain a Who's Whoess.

WOOLSEY, Cardinal, a churchman who combined politics with his profession, became wealthy, unfortunate, and was finally written up by Shakespeare.

WRIGHT, Orville, one of the inventors of the aeroplane who knows the inside of the business, and believes one life on the ground is worth two in the air.

CHAPTER X[1]

XENOPHON, a Greek who endeavored to introduce morals into his country. He died young.

XYLOPHONES, inventor of the xylophone.

---

[1] Ed. Note: The editor is again compelled to apologize for the X's.

CHAPTER Y

YALE, Eli, founder of the enemy of Harvard and Princeton. Football, pipe, and bulldog fancier.

YORICK, an acquaintance of Hamlet who was recognized even in an emaciated condition.

YOUNG, Brigham, the man who introduced Mohammedanism into the United States and placed Utah on the flag. When a young man he became a strong anti-monogamist. Moved west with his wives. Utah increased in population and was admitted as a state. After building a great temple, dedicated to Hymen, he died, leaving a considerable family and a few widows. Heirs: See Utah census. Ambition: London and New York in Utah. Address: Utah. Clubs: Race Suicide. Epitaph: Like Father, Like Son.

CHAPTER Z

ZANGWELL, Israel, a child of the Ghetto who believed the pen was more profitable than the pack. Ambition: The Promised Utopia. Recreation: Zangwell plays. Address: The Ghetto. Clubs: A. O. H.

ZANY, A., the book reviewer who said Who Was Who was the greatest book ever written.

ZEPPELIN, Ferdinand, manufacturer of wrecked dirigibles, and an aeronaut who knew how to land. Insurance still in vogue. Ambition: The elevation of the German army. Recreation: Aeronautics with the Kaiser. Address: Air. Clubs: Aero.

ZOROASTER. He was the man who introduced fires into warm countries. He also thanks the readers in the name of the Editor for their kind attention.

www.ingramcontent.com/pod-product-compliance
Lightning Source LLC
Chambersburg PA
CBHW051550010526
44118CB00022B/2649